Coming
Clean

Coming Clean

Rodney Carrington

with Bret Witter

CENTER
STREET®

NEW YORK BOSTON NASHVILLE

Center Street
Hachette Book Group USA
237 Park Avenue
New York, NY 10017

Visit our Web site at www.centerstreet.com.

Center Street is a division of Hachette Book Group USA, Inc. The Center
Street name and logo is a trademark of Hachette Book Group USA, Inc.

Printed in the United States of America

First Edition: September 2007
10 9 8 7 6 5 4 3 2 1

Library of Congress Cataloging-in-Publication Data

Carrington, Rodney.
  Coming clean / by Rodney Carrington with Bret Witter. — 1st ed.
    p. cm.
  "Chart-topping comedian Rodney Carrington offers up his first
book helping of the Texas-sized, down-home humor that has sold out
his comedy tour across the nation"—Provided by the publisher.
  ISBN-13: 978-1-59995-702-9
  ISBN-10: 1-59995-702-7
  1. American wit and humor. I. Witter, Bret. II. Title.
  PN6165.C366 2007
  818'.602—dc22   2007006723

Contents

CONTENTS

CONTENTS

Acknowledgments

So many people helped me with this book that I couldn't thank them all in twenty-five pages, much less one. For that reason, I'm going to mention just three indispensable people: my editor, Chris Park, who pushed me to go back and make the book better (three times!); my good friend Mark Gross, whose insights and humor punched up the comedy and made most of the dull chapters interesting; and my writer, Bret Witter, who took the stories I've been telling for years and turned them into a book. And of course, I wouldn't be writing this book if it wasn't for you, the reader; thank you very much for caring. I truly appreciate it.

A Note from the Writer

My name is Bret Witter. I'm a thirty-five-year-old, six-foot-tall Caucasian male. I live in Louisville, Kentucky, with my wife, Elizabeth, and my three-year-old daughter, Lydia, who is the greatest person who has ever lived.

I love bluegrass music, straw hats, pepperoni pizza, Budweiser out of the can, and crawfish étouffée with hibiscus-marmalade sauce.

I can jump over a John Deere riding lawn mower, swim the Ohio River (the short way), and kick the ass of a thirteenth-degree magenta belt in to-fu-yun (did it last week). I built my own house out of Lincoln logs. Colored every page of a Barney coloring book without once going over the line. Did I mention I was the original oboe player for Ronnie James Dio? And just this morning I baked the first completely vegan tiramisu.

But that's my personal life. In my professional life, I'm a ghostwriter, which means I help write books . . . for other people. I'm the guy that went to Rodney's house and helped him organize his notes. And every letter that appears on every one of these pages—I typed it.

Most authors pretend I don't exist. They say, "Thanks, Bret. We'll put your name in the acknowledgments." How many people read the acknowledgments? I thought so.

But Rodney is different. Rodney wants people to know I was involved. Of course, with great power comes great responsibility. Now I'm on the hook. Not legally or financially (that's in my contract), but morally.

So if you find anything in this book that is untrue, poorly written, utterly stupid, moronically trite, horribly unfunny, personally offensive, or just plain wrong—that's my fault, and I apologize.

Everything else—that's Rodney.

So without wasting any more time, let me bring out the man you've all come here to read, the headlining act, the singing cowboy, the guy who shot a guy who shot a guy named Fred, the funniest man you'll ever want to share a beer with, and the next president of the Hell's Angels, Tulsa Chapter . . . Mr. Rodney Carrington.

"If Sam Kinison and Hank Williams, Jr., had a baby, he'd grow up to be Rodney Carrington."

Bob & Tom

Coming Clean

HANGIN' WITH RODNEY

Hi. I'm Rodney Carrington. I'm a comedian from Longview, Texas. That's in Texas. I live with my family in Tulsa, Oklahoma. That's in Oklahoma. Before we get too intimate, I thought it might be a good idea to tell you a little bit about myself. So put your panties back on and listen up for a minute.

I like George Jones and Frank Sinatra, but not necessarily in that order. I like a quiet night out with my family, just dinner and a movie. If I have a beer, it's no more than six, and usually more like two. If I have a fancy drink, it's a frozen strawberry margarita. I'm not ashamed; there ain't nothing wrong with it.

I like cowboy boots. I've worn them all my life. But I'm not a cowboy. I have 194 acres and four dogs, but I don't ride horses or know anything about cattle. I drive a truck, but that doesn't mean I'm hauling manure to the back forty. My favorite leisure activity is golf.

I don't like people who don't like things. I don't like people who like to talk about not liking things. Life's short. Why be negative? Of course, I hate beets. I don't even like people that like beets, that's how much I hate them.

People sometimes accuse me of being blue, meaning my humor is on the cutting edge. But I'm not blue, I'm true. People sometimes accuse me of being red, as in a redneck. But I'm not red, I'm suburban country. People sometimes accuse me of being white. But . . . well, that is true. I'm white.

The reason all this is even mildly important is that this book is about me. I'm not a comic that does observational humor. I don't say, "You know what's weird? Every time you go to the urinal in a public bathroom, there's piss on the floor. Who the hell misses the urinal?" (In case you're wondering, ladies, that is true. There is always piss on the floor in men's bathrooms. We are disgusting creatures.)

My humor is about my life. I tell stories about myself, my wife, my kids, and my friends. I figure if it's happened to me, it's probably happened to you; let's all drink beer and laugh at ourselves for a while.

If you like my comedy, you're going to like this book. But since reading is a lot harder than listening, I've thought long and hard about the best way to make this experience as painless as possible for both of us.

My first idea was a coloring book. I'd color in the pictures, then you could just cut them out and stick them on your refrigerator.

Then I thought of a bunch of naked pictures of women, but I found out they already have those kinds of publications. They're called porno magazines.

Next I tried "Rodney's Pamphlet." Fifteen pages long, so it should only take you five visits to the shitter to get through it.

Finally, I came up with this book, which has a lot of words in it, but at least I've kept the chapters short. Since you're going to be wasting a lot of time reading, I even included an important lesson. But just one. And near the back. Anything else you learn from this book is completely by accident. I apologize in advance.

My father always tells me, "I cannot believe you get paid to drink beer and give people your opinion on things. I've been doing that all my life, and nobody's every paid me a dime."

My sixth-grade teacher put it a different way. One day, I decided to turn in an English test without answering any of the questions. Instead, on the bottom of the test, I drew a picture of a donkey with a human head and a big turd coming out of its behind. Underneath the picture I wrote: Shit a brick.

I did it because I was bored, and I thought it would be funny. Apparently I was wrong, because Ms. Anderson wasn't laughing when she jerked me out of class and said: "You cannot always be a disruption, Rodney Carrington. You cannot just do what you want all your life. You cannot make a living entertaining people with crude humor."

Fortunately, Ms. Anderson was wrong. I've made a living out of entertaining people. And the reason is you. All you people who have seen my shows and bought my albums and even bought this book—you've given me the greatest gift in the world: your time.

So thank you to my fans—all two of you. Larry, Curly, I really appreciate it. And from here until the end of this book, I'm going to try as hard as I can to tell it like it is and make you laugh.

"When you write a book, they tell you to start with something truly important and meaningful, so here goes nothing . . ."

THE BEST THINGS IN LIFE

There are a lot of great things in life, but there are two that really stand out for me: boobs. I like boobs. I'm a man, I like titties, I can't help it, that's how we are.

If you don't want to read about titties . . . well, I'm not sure why you chose this book. But just in case there's been some misunderstanding, I'm going to make it easy for you. I'm going to get the titty discussion out of the way right here in this chapter. If you don't like it, just skip right ahead. There's some good shit up there, too.

The story starts in the summer of 1992. I was in Orlando, Florida. I'd been on the road awhile, didn't have much money, didn't have much to do, and the hotel owner told me there was a place down the road where they kept the boobs. It's called a titty bar. You go in there, sit down, they bring them out a few at a time and show them to you. You can compare makes and models, see the new colors, check out the hood ornaments. It's kind of like a used-car dealership, except when you choose a few you like they tell you, "Sorry, sir, they're not actually for sale. We're charging you just for looking and that will be four hundred dollars."

I jumped in a truck with some stranger from the hotel bar and headed over. We came over the hill and suddenly there it was—the blinding light of glory!—a building in the shape of two big old titties. I've never been so happy to see a building in all my life. It was like the Wizard of Oz for grown men. You come up over that hill and, "My god, Johnny, there it is, just like the little people said it would be."

We got out of the truck, held hands, skipped up to the door. A little midget answered and said, "Can I help you?"

"You damn sure can. We came to see the wizard. Is she here?"

Well, that's not exactly how it happened. Actually, I skipped up to the door and said, "So . . . is this the doughnut shop?" The big bouncer rolled his eyes. He'd heard them all before. I went in, sat down in the left titty . . . and somehow spent my whole paycheck in about two hours.

Which in those days was $158.23. Yep, I tipped her with pennies.

That's the problem with titty clubs. You stare at titties for two hours, you get dumber than a box of shit. But that doesn't mean you don't like it. I've never met a titty I didn't like. Get me around titties, I'm like a woman in a shoe store. "I want to see every pair of them sonofabitches, get them out here. Yes, even the mismatched pairs."

Titties are a temptation, I'm not going to tell you they're not. Did you know there are two of those things for every woman on the planet? That's a lot, lot, lot of temptation.

On the other hand, titties make you honest. You just cannot lie to your woman when you've been to a titty bar. You come in the front door, smelling of cheap cigarettes and even cheaper perfume, and she's waiting for you.

"Where you been?"

Hee-hee. "Titty bar."

"How much did you spend?"

Umm. "About nine thousand."

"Where's your truck?"

"They got that, too."

"Where's your clothes?"

"I'm not real sure."

"Who's she?

"Hell, honey, I thought she was you."

Whatever you got coming to you then, it's fair. You deserve it. That's another great thing about titties: no bullshit. A man and a woman will always get right to the important issues when titties are involved.

Another important thing about titties, at least when the conversation isn't about how you screwed up and touched the wrong one, is that they're calming. I realized that one day while I was out with my good friend Mark Gross. We were walking down the street, having a conversation, and suddenly a gorgeous woman in a tight white T-shirt walked by. We both just stopped talking and started smiling. Whatever we were saying, it just went right out of our heads—and in came happy.

When there are titties around, you can't think of anything but titties. You start planning how to get closer to them. Look at them. Touch them. Maybe even lick them. Then you realize you're in Sears with your wife and kids, those are somebody else's titties, and it's never going to happen.

Which is one of the reasons I think titties are underestimated. I just can't see a bunch of men sitting down and deciding to go to war if there are titties in the room. I'm not talking about women, because they can get just as wound up as men; I'm talking about titties. How can you stay mad when there are titties around?

And banana splits. There is no way to be angry when you are eating a banana split. If you called a meeting, and that meeting had titties and banana splits, there is no way you would come out of that room wanting to hurt somebody. Not going to happen; can't be done.

You see, it's not the presence of titties that's the problem—ever. You can't ever blame the titties. The problem is what happens when someone takes them away. Anger is what happens when the bar closes, you're cold, you're drunk, you're all alone, and they just took you for the baby formula money.

Which is why, to tell you the truth, I've never really been a fan of titty bars. They aren't a big part of my life, and they never have been. If you like them, and you can look responsibly, then have at it. I'm not judging you. But, personally, I haven't been to a titty bar since . . . actually, I can't remember the last time I went to a titty bar. I love titties, don't get me wrong, I just do not have a desire to pay to see them on display.

I'm a husband now. I'm the father of three boys. I try not to go anywhere or do anything that would be embarrassing in front of my kids. What if my oldest boy came into a titty bar and saw me staring at a barely dressed twenty-year-old? That's when the excuses would fly.

"What's going on here? Where am I? I thought this was the doughnut shop."

"Titties? I didn't even notice those titties. I was just having a beer."

"I think I've been abducted. I was on the way to the store for milk and . . . well, something must have grabbed the wheel."

I'd point to some bald-headed pervert and say, "It wasn't my idea. He made me come. I hate it in here."

"Hey, wait a minute. What's a ten-year-old doing in a titty bar?"

I'd look around real fast. "Where's your mother, Zach? Oh

no, don't tell me. Please don't tell me. She's at it again, isn't she? She's at the bingo parlor. With the church ladies. Knitting sweaters for orphans. She's so selfish."

About that time I'd probably start thinking, *Hell, we're all here now, what's the harm in one more beer?*

Then I'd see my son staring at those titties, and my dad instinct would kick in. I'd put my arm around him and say, "Come on now, son. Get in the truck. I'll buy you some chicken wings and curly fries. And if your mom ever asks what we did tonight, you tell her I took you down to a construction site to strip copper wire for scrap."

SLIP 'n SLIDE

I grew up in Texas in the 1970s. It was a more innocent time. It was a time when an eight-year-old could still ride his bike down to the Dairy Queen and buy a pack of cigarettes from the vending machine. Which I did.

For two months, I'd ride down every week and sample another flavor. "Hmm, I think I'll try the brown ones. Kool. That sounds good." I'd take the cigarettes up to my room and smoke them with the window open. Then one day I got cocky and walked into the kitchen with a box of Laughy Taffy and a cigarette hanging out of my eight-year-old lips. All I remember is the sound of the phone dropping out of my mother's hand and hitting the floor.

It wasn't just the cancer that bothered her; it was also the waste of money. Because we were poor. I didn't know that then, but I know it now. Actually, I wasn't poor, my mom was poor; she just dragged my ass along with her.

You remember slip and slide? Big yellow piece of plastic, hurts on gravel. I didn't have a slip-and-slide. I had two Hefty garbage bags taped together. You'd slide two seconds, do a face plant in the dirt. "All right! That was a good 'un. Your turn, Billy!"

We'd be out with no shirt, no shoes, just our Toughskins jeans. If there is one thing that says country boy, it is wearing Toughskins jeans with no shirt.

I don't know if you remember Toughskins, but in 1976 they were every kid's worst nightmare. They were thick, dark blue, and hot as hell in the summer. It was like wearing a carpet on your legs. The only good thing about them was that they were the closest a poor kid could ever get to body armor. You couldn't burn a hole in those jeans. Believe me, I tried lighters, firecrackers, kerosene, cat urine, just about everything to get out of wearing Toughskins. Those jeans were indestructible. I believe if President Kennedy had been wearing a hat made out of Toughskins jeans he'd still be with us today.

I hope that one didn't turn you off. I told that one a few times in my stage show and people actually booed. I still can't believe it. The man's been gone forty years, and some people act like you went fishing with him yesterday.

Whether or not Toughskins would have saved a president's life—and I think at the very least Lee Harvey Oswald would have misfired he'd have been laughing so hard at those jeans hanging off the back of Kennedy's head—they did save many a kid from horrible injury. No matter how hard you slid off the end of that Hefty bag, and no matter how much gravel ended up embedded in your forehead, your Toughskins would come away looking just like they did the day your mom bought them at Sears. Which basically means that no matter what you did, your Toughskins always looked like shit.

COUNTRY

I wasn't just poor when I was growing up, I was also country. I lived in the kind of place where your neighbors are always having Vietnam flashbacks. And they'd never even been to Vietnam. "Get down. I can smell him."

"Smell what?"

"Deer."

"Of course you can. You're lying in deer shit."

We had guys that would come to school bragging about the hunt. "Killed a deer this weekend. He snuck up on me, I couldn't get to my gun, so I beat him with a stick. Rode him three miles, chased him another two, finally broke his antler off and stabbed him through the heart with it three times."

I'm not a hunter. I do not like the idea of getting up at four-thirty in the morning in the middle of winter, just so I can sit in a tree for six hours hoping an animal walks by. If I have to kill a deer, my instrument of choice is a Buick. You paint it camouflage, hide it in the bushes, turn on the radio to easy listening, and wait.

"There he is, Rodney. We got him. Just start her up real slow."

I've been all over the United States now, so I know the country isn't just in Texas, it's everywhere. You should see them down in Mississippi; they don't even touch their lips together when they talk.

You walk into a convenience store in Mississippi, the guy says, "Kin a hep yu."

"Get your finger out of your nose and you might. I'm taking these here Cheetos and no thank you, don't bag it for me, that's all right. And keep the change. I don't want to touch that either."

Then there are the empty states, like Nebraska. There ain't a tree, there ain't a lake, there ain't a bush. They've got sleds but no hills, it don't make any sense.

All they've got in Nebraska is a bunch of tractors and some nice thick women. It's not their fault; they're just wearing their winter coats—on the inside. I'm pretty sure some of them played football for the University of Nebraska, we just couldn't tell they were women because of the mustaches.

Oh, and corn. There is corn everywhere in Nebraska. There is corn where there should never, ever, be corn. Believe me, I've seen it. Once or twice, I've even thought about trying it. But it's so damn bumpy.

All you can do in states like Nebraska is drink and farm, farm and drink, and then go to the comedy club and make fun of some boy from out of town. I think those Nebraska farmers come to the club just to see if they can make you cry. They say, "I'm pissed. You pissed? Good, let's go down to the comedy club and humiliate some poor bastard."

And Nebraska's not the only state like that. There are a lot of small towns out there in America, and I've visited most of them. I'm talking about towns with one airport: Ed's airport, which is an old Wal-Mart with a grass runway out back. They've got a tube sock hanging off a pole to tell which way the wind is blowing. The only airline—Ed's airline—makes you sit in lawn chairs. The only hotel in town—Ed's hotel, the same bastard that flies the airplane—is a trailer. The shower only has one stream of water coming out of it. It's like a dog peeing on your back, which is like a horse peeing on your back, only softer.

If you've never had a horse pee on your back, well then, you're not really from the country.

SMALL-TOWN RESTAURANTS

Denny's—now that's a terrible restaurant. Every time I go to Denny's, it's like going before the judge to be sentenced. I'm pretty confident that I am about to lose three years off my life.

There used to be a Denny's in every small town in America, so I went there a lot when I was on the road. I'd walk in alone and the hostess would say: "How many?"

I'd look around—nope, still nobody but me—and I'd want to ask, "What does it feel like to be a complete idiot?"

But that poor hostess has enough problems. You ever see a woman so scary she makes you jump back and say, "Oh, shit"? She probably works at Denny's.

And those uniforms aren't helping. I don't know who decided on brown polyester, but he ought to be forced to eat thirty-nine Grand Slam breakfasts every day for the rest of his life. Those tight brown pants bunch up the fat; all the women have dimples on their ass. It looks like they've been hit in the back of the legs with a bag of nickels. By the time you get to your table, you've lost your appetite.

The country is changing, though. Instead of a Denny's, now every small town has a Chinese restaurant. It's usually called Poontang.

"Where-you-want-sit?"

"Hey, slow down there, Kung Pao. It's not like you've got anything to do. It's a buffet."

"What-you-want-eat?"

"Whoa, let me look at the menu. Let's see. My wife will have the moo goo guy pan, because it's the only thing she can pronounce. I'll take the poontang."

"You want poontang. Good choice, cowboy."

I got to admit, I like the poontang.

Then there are those restaurants where they cook the food in front of you. I think they're Japanese, but I'm not sure and I don't really give a shit. It's good food, and it's a good time. The problem is that half the time some jackass hillbilly like me shows up to cook.

"What happened, Billy Bob? Where's Ching Lee?"

It's like going to Disneyland and having Chuck E. Cheese filling in for Mickey Mouse. You don't want a substitute, you want the real thing. If I go to one of those restaurants, I want the Japanese guy that comes out with a big yell: "Hiiiy-yaaa!" He throws a knife, kills the guy next to him. "He don't work here no more."

"No shit, Kung-Fu. He's dead."

Here's a million-dollar idea: Instead of just having the Japanese share their culture with us, we should share our culture with them, too. Some hillbilly should open a chain of restaurants in Japanese where we cook in front of them—our way. Four lawn chairs, a bug zapper, a big old grill, and a cowboy in a dirty apron saying, "What's it going to be, Hirohito, hot dog or hamburger?"

ME AND THE
RED-HEADED FAT KID

Nobody participated in anything at my high school. We barely had enough people for football, and you can forget about competitive chess. It got so bad, my junior year the coach just randomly assigned people to run track. He comes up to me one day, hands me a uniform, and says, "Congratulations, Carrington, you made the team."

The uniform is a green polyester hand-me-down that hasn't been washed in ten years. I had to wear a jockstrap just to keep from catching herpes. The shorts are so tight you got one nut hanging over each side of the seam. I get to the meet and notice all the guys are bouncing around, so I figure that's part of the warm-up. I try it, but it hurts like hell. It's like someone's juggling my nuts down there.

"Carrington, you're running the four hundred meters."

"What's that, coach?"

"I don't know. Hold on a second." He consults some papers. "It's one time around the track."

"Do you have any advice?"

"Just run as fast as you can."

So I take off running. They chase me down and tell me I have to wait for the starting gun, which sucks, because I was way out in front.

So I come back to the line, jump around a few times, tuck my nuts back into my green pants, get down in a crouch, and as soon as I hear the starting gun I take off in a dead sprint. And I'm way out in front. I'm so far out in front I think I'm awesome. I'm the shortest, whitest guy in the whole meet, and I am going to win.

Then I hit the third corner and a gorilla jumps on my back. Suddenly, it's like I'm carrying four people. I take two more steps, and everybody passes me like I am standing still. Shit. I'm not awesome. I suck.

At that point, I do the only reasonable thing. I pull up, grab my hamstring, limp off the track, and head straight for the concession stand. I'm halfway through a large Coke and a package of Sprees when the coach catches up to me.

"What happened, Carrington?"

"Got a cramp, coach."

"Damn. You were killing them for the first half of the race. Next week you run the two hundred meters."

I look around the next week, and I don't even match up. There are seven long, tall, athletic-looking guys and one short white guy shaped like a block of cheese. I've only taken four steps before the winner is across the finish line. At least it was only half the distance to humiliation.

But the coach won't give up on me. He says, "Look, Carrington, you're slow as hell, but you've got heart. I'm going to put you in the mile."

And I'm excited. I'm excited because I show up the next week and there are thirty-seven people entered in the mile. I

figure with that many people, there's no way I'm going to finish last again.

There are two twins from my school running the mile with
me, and they tell me, "The mile is easy. Just stick with us."

The mile is not easy. It may seem easy when you're driving
a truck down to the Quik-e-Mart for some Budweiser tallboys,
but when you're using your feet it's a hell of a long way. The
twins apparently didn't know this, because they take off running
at three-quarters sprint speed. I'm like "Guys . . . guys . . ."
We're ten feet into the race and I'm already having trouble
talking and running at the same time. "You . . . you guys going
to run this fast the whole time?"

"Yeah, just stick with us."

"Yeah . . . I . . . I think I'm going to drop back a little bit.
I'll . . . I'll catch up later."

That seemed to work. I looked back after a lap, and I'm in
the middle of the pack. Hell yes, I'll take mediocre.

Then one guy passes me. Fine. Don't worry. He's an
overachiever.

Then another guy passes me. Fine.

Then another. Wait a second.

We get to the last lap, and there are only eight people behind me. They're still passing me, one by one, and there is
nothing I can do about it. My brain is going, *You've got to*, but
my body is saying, *But we can't.*

Finally, it comes down to me and the red-headed fat kid.
And I'm bargaining. I say to him, "Look, let's run in together.
It won't be as bad that way. We'll finish together as if we were
just doing this for the exercise."

He says, "Okay, okay, sure." I'm thinking I've not only
solved my problem, but I've made a new friend. I'm happy. I
can barely breathe, but I'm happy.

We get to the last hundred meters, and the red-headed fat

kid takes off in a dead sprint. I can't believe it. He sold me out. The fat kid sold me out. Sure, I was going to sell him out, but I was going to be a gentleman and wait until the last ten meters.

No matter what you're doing, there is one rule that always holds water. When the red-headed fat kid outsmarts you, it's time to quit.

LEE GREENWOOD'S HAIR

I didn't grow up with money. I didn't have a giant inheritance coming or a rich relative anywhere in my family. Like a lot of poor kids, I thought money would solve all my problems. And I knew that if I was ever going to have money, I was going to have to make it myself.

My stepdad Jimmy owned a barber college, so when I was fifteen he took me in the back room, pulled out a creepy dummy head, and showed me how to cut hair. Snip this. Cut that. Watch out for the ear. Two minutes into the demonstration a guy walked into the shop and Jimmy said, "Cut his hair."

"What?"

"You're ready."

"But I don't know what I'm doing."

"Don't worry. It's just hair."

I thought about it and figured he was right. It wasn't like I was doing boob jobs; that's a procedure no guy wants to screw up. They'll shoot you for screwing up boobs.

Barbers are guys named Red or Scooter. They have nick-names. A barber sits you down in the chair and says, "My name's Johnny, but everybody calls me Scissors." It makes you feel good, because you know Scissors is just like you.

You don't want a surgeon with a nickname. You don't want your surgeon to be just like you. You want him to be smart and give a shit. The last thing you want to hear before you go under the knife is, "Hi, I'm Ernie, but you can call me Clumsy. I'll be doing your brain today."

When I'm dealing with a pilot or a surgeon, I want them to have a serious name, like Steubing Redford. Something manly and rich. A little more information on their life would be nice, too. I'd like to walk on the airplane and be handed a card with a short biography of the guy who's going to have my life in his hands for the next six hours.

> Hello, and welcome to Asshole Airlines. Your pilot today is Ramsey "Ramrod" Davenport. He's from Connecti-cut and went to private school, where he was known for wrestling pythons and bedding townies. He spent three years in the Navy shooting down Russian jets and air-dropping relief supplies to Nebraska. Ramrod is married with two children and a dog named Boo. His interests include sensual massage, fast cars, single malt Scotch whiskey, and lots of it. In fact, he's an alcoholic. He's probably drunk right now. Have a nice flight!

Barbers are a different breed. You read the bio of a barber, it says:

> Red has been a barber for twenty-three years. He grew up in this town. He's divorced.

Once I thought about that, I figured I had what it takes to be a barber. And I did. My first customer was reasonably happy. My second customer was a hobo. He was a long-haired, long-bearded, scraggly-looking fella. Just washing his hair made a difference. Then I cut his hair short and trimmed his beard. When I was done, I looked down . . . and it was Lee Greenwood.

It made me proud to be a barber,
so I gave him that cut for free.
Now he won't forget the man who dyes,
and gave that trim to him.

Actually, it wasn't Lee Greenwood, but it sure looked like Lee Greenwood. I said, "Man, you look like Lee Greenwood." He looked at himself in the mirror and said, "You're right. I do." That is the most excited I have ever seen anyone get about a haircut.

Then a ten-year-old kid came in. "Hey mister, can you trim my burr?"

"Sure, Beaver Cleaver. Just step into the cockpit here, Ace, and I'll fix you right up."

I pulled the electric shears on him, and I'll be damned if I didn't accidentally touch his scalp and put a line in the side of his head. I looked over to the guy next to me and said, "What do I do, Rick? I just put a line on his head."

Rick looked at me, looked at the kid's hair, and said, "Put a line on the other side. Make it look like you did it on purpose."

The kid's mom came in five minutes later and saw what I'd done. Her boy had racing stripes. That was the end of my barbering career.

AMWAY

When I was a senior in high school, I paid $150 and became an Amway salesman. The idea behind Amway is that you buy stuff you need, like shampoo and toilet paper, in bulk at discount prices. It's like Costco, except you buy it from yourself and you have to wait six weeks to get it. It didn't make any damn sense.

But it wasn't really about selling yourself toilet paper. It was about getting other people to sell themselves toilet paper. Amway had a pitch: "Do you have six friends?"

"Of course."

"Then you can make an extra $150 a month. Do each of those friends have six friends?"

"Probably."

"Then you can make an extra $650 a month."

And so on, and so on, and after about five minutes all I saw were dollar signs. If you had a lot of friends, which I did, it seemed like you were going to be a millionaire.

So I buy a suit at Sears, and I drive my mother's car down

to the big Amway meeting in Dallas. I'm holding hands with strangers, singing songs, people are crying. I'm so moved I want to get up and give a speech. "Yes we can! Yes we can!" But I haven't done anything yet. I don't even know what we're supposed to be doing.

I get home, and I call all my friends and tell them to come over right away, I got some big shit going on. I put on my Sears suit and, just like they told me at the revival, I put a pot of coffee and a box of doughnuts out on the kitchen table, even though it's the middle of the afternoon.

My friends show up. They're just high-school students. They've got their ball caps on backward, dipping, saying, "What's goin' on, man?"

I'm shaking hands with them at the door, wearing my suit. "Come on in, fellas. Welcome. Welcome. You want some coffee?"

I've got a big easel board set up, and I start right in on the pitch. "Gentlemen, you have just entered the Billionaire's Club. Your lives are about to change. I have found the secret golden grail, and I am going to share it with you today. You are going to thank me forever. Now . . . do you have six friends?"

"Yeah. We're all in this room, dumbass."

"That's very funny. Ha, ha. But seriously, do you have six friends?"

"Why are you wearing a suit? You look like a moron."

"Okay, fine, I know you have six friends. Now would you like to earn an extra $150 a month?"

"Hell yeah. Where do we get it? Yee-haw."

I can't believe it. They're heckling me. I've just learned the secret of the universe, and I'm trying to share it with my best friends, and they're laughing at me. But I push on. I've felt the Amway love; I know I can make this work.

"If you've got six friends, and they've each got six friends . . ."

"What is this about, gathering friends? What's the point?"

"I'm getting to it. Shut up." Now I'm getting mad. I cannot believe how wrong things are going. I mean, this is Amway!

"Hey, man, this coffee's getting cold. You got any beer?"

"And these doughnuts suck. Why didn't you get crullers?"

"That's it! Get out! I'm up here trying to change your lives. I'm trying to make you rich. And you don't give a shit. So get out!"

Then I turn on my girlfriend, who's been laughing along with my friends. "And you. I told you to wear a dress, and you show up in cut-off jeans. I mean, they're hot. My god, you are hot. But I am trying to be professional here."

At that point, most people would have a revelation. They'd see how stupid they're being and give it up. But not me. I was too far gone. I decide I was going to prove them wrong. I was going to make that million dollars. I was going to do it.

"Yes I can! Yes I can!"

I buy Dale Carnegie's book, *The Seven Highly Infectious Dwarves*, or whatever the hell it's called. I start wearing my suit to weird places, like the mall. And I start selling, selling, selling. One day two twelve-year-old boys from the Longview Baptist Temple came to our door. They said, "If you died today, would you go to heaven?"

I said, "Come on in, boys. I'd like to show you something. You ever heard of Amway?" Half an hour later a lady pops up at the door, real worried, asking if we have seen two young men. I'm still back there selling. Those boys came with God and left with the religion of Amway.

Six months of hard work later, I'm lying in the back of my truck, in shorts, in the sun, reading Dale Carnegie's book. The mailman pulls up with my first check from Amway. It's for $3.68. I turned around and threw the check and the Dale Carnegie book in the trash.

I learned a valuable lesson that day: If you're going to start acting like an asshole millionaire, at least make some money first.

BREAKFAST CEREAL

I love women. Big, little, black, white, round, square, purple triangles, green clovers, blue diamonds, I love them all, and not just because their chest is the place God chose to store the titties.

I love women because they're calming. No, wait, that's the titties. Women aren't calming. Women make you crazy. That hairy critter in their britches causes more trouble than anything else in this world. If that isn't true, then why was the first war in written history called the Trojan War?

Vaginas are powerful things. They're like magnets that suck all the common sense out of a man's head and into his nether regions. You don't think so? Try this, all you women out there. Stop having sex with your man for a week, then throw a can of wet, sticky, rancid dog food out in front yard and tell your man, "If you go out there in the yard and eat that dog food you can have some." He'll be back five minutes later with a beef-flavored ring around his mouth.

"I did it!"

"You nasty sonofabitch, I was kidding."

"But you promised."

"Yeah, but now you smell like Alpo."

Women have power. I should know, I grew up with a mom, three sisters, and no dad. Even the dog was a girl. Actually, it wasn't all female around my house. I did have a dad growing up. In fact, I had five of them, but they were the kind you borrow for a while, like library books. Read them once, get bored, send them back. My mom married my soccer coach. She married my barber. That's no joke, it's a fact.

Growing up with women, you learn a few things. Like the word *twat*, the most nonsexy word ever created to describe the vagina. That is the only word that can turn me off when it comes to the privates. A woman can say, "Do you want to see my twat?" and I'm going to honestly answer, "Not if you put it that way I don't."

"Would you like to see me squat with my twat?"

"Not if you . . . well, actually, hell yes, I'd love to."

I learned that word because my mother would always tell my sisters. "Get in that bathroom and clean your twat." I didn't know what that meant until I was seventeen. I just kept going in the shower and thinking, *Okay, where's the twat? I'll clean it, for god's sake, I'm tired of the bitching.*

Then I found out what it was. I'd get all smiley and giggly, kind of like the slow kid in class, and say, "I like twat. It's my favorite."

Of course, it took me another ten years to figure out that big water bottle with the long hose hanging in the shower. First, I thought it was a squirt gun. Then I thought it was a balloon, but you can't blow that sonofabitch up, you'll bust a blood vessel in your head.

Do you know what I'm talking about? I'm talking about douche, people. Pooty-poo cleaner.

Douche doesn't come in those squirt bottles anymore. Now it comes in a regular bottle. Smells like country flower, or at least that's what the label says. What kind of flavor is country flower? Who wants to eat a country flower? Please, Massengail, make a flavor we like: chicken, beef bouillon. Give me a reason to take my hat off and go down there.

Eventually, with a man, everything leads back to sex. Boss. Work. Car. Dinner. Chicken. Douche. Pussy. Sex! That's because pussy is our friend. I'm a man and I think about it every single second of every single day.

A lot of you women are probably going, "Not my man." Bullshit. I don't care if he wears a white collar to work on Sunday and carries a Bible, he's thinking about pussy. Right now. Go ahead, look at him. See that little smile in the corner of his mouth? Pussy.

If you don't think there's a difference between men and women, think about this. If you created a cereal called Pussy Puffs, you'd make a fortune. Men would be lined up out the door waiting to buy some Pussy Puffs.

You couldn't convince a woman to buy a cereal called Dick-a-Roos. Shaped like a penis, tastes like sugar.

Well, all right, that might work. But unlike men, women wouldn't be lining up for it. They'd be buying it off the Internet, hiding it on a back shelf, and enjoying it alone.

THE TRUTH ABOUT SPORTS

I don't know how many times I've had women tell me, "All you ever do is think about sex, you disgusting pervert." And I'm talking about those hairy women down at the driver's license office. You should hear my poor gorgeous wife. She has to use a can of Raid, an aluminum baseball bat, and a naked picture of Jerry Springer to keep me away from her. And that's just when we're shopping at Wal-Mart.

Of course, I've got a suspicion. I suspect women think about sex all the time, just like men. There's a billion-dollar industry out there for dildos, and somebody's using them. In fact, I've caught my wife leaning up against the washing machine while it was vibrating a whole bunch of times.

"What you doing, honey?"

"F-f-f-f-folding laundry."

"Looks like it feels pretty good."

"Oh-h-h-h yeah."

"Umm . . . can I watch?"

Yep, that joke's going to scar my three kids for life, but

they're boys, they need to know the truth. Women like sex. Women like sex, but they are emotional creatures. They like to think things over, give them some meaning, have them matter. If they didn't, we'd all be in a big naked pile right now and we'd be having a whole lot of fun.

That's why men created sports, so we can think about sex without having to involve the women. Sex is all about finding the girl, getting to the spot, putting it in the hole. Find her, get there, score. That's sports, too.

Football: uprights, right through the middle. Basketball: five guys fighting five other guys to score. It's just like being in a nightclub.

Golf. Now that's my game. Nothing makes me hornier than golf. It's just like getting ready for sex. You've got your bag out, you're washing your balls, and you've got your stick in your hand. You get ready to take your first shot, and you've got three friends there criticizing your form.

"Keep your head down, dumbass."

"Tuck your elbow. Don't forget to rotate your hips."

"Quit biting your bottom lip. You look like you're trying to get the lid off a jar of pickles."

You take your first shot, and you're feeling pretty good about it until someone says, "Hell yeah, looks like you got some solid wood on that one. Too bad it's headed for the wrong hole."

The only real difference between sex and golf is that with golf, you want to get done in as few strokes as possible. In golf, if I can finish in under eighty strokes, I'm happy. With sex, I'm just praying to get to fifteen.

Tennis: Now that's a different story. Tennis was clearly invented by a woman because that's just arguing. Back and forth, back and forth, back and forth. Will somebody shut up already and hit the ball into the net, my wife said I could get some as soon as this damn match is over and you are taking forever!

THE KING OF COMEDY

People think I have the best job in the world. I walk on stage, talk about bullshit for forty-five minutes, drink a few beers, say "Good night," and head for the shower. I've got to admit, it's better than bolting tires on the assembly line or driving an eighteen-wheeler full of cabbage. Hell, it might just be the best job in the world.

But it wasn't always like that. I didn't wake up one morning, walk downstairs, and find two thousand people in my living room waiting for me to entertain them. It's not like I looked down at my bathrobe, coffee in hand, and said, "Oh, morning wood. How about I sing you guys a little song about that?"

No, it started in a little lounge called Sparky's, which was next to the lobby of the Park Inn Hotel just outside Longview. A comedian was doing a bit about the Village People and he asked for volunteers. Me and my buddy got up on stage dressed like gay Indians and people started laughing.

I thought, *This is easy. I can do this.* So when Sparky's announced an amateur night, I signed up for ten minutes. I was so scared that first night I drank sixty-three bourbon and Cokes and a piña colada. Then I did Elvis impersonations. I wore a fake nose. I did an over-the-top soul man in a big afro wig singing the national anthem.

I ended up getting hired as the MC at Sparky's. I'd say a few words between acts, tell a few jokes, introduce the real comedians. And I got paid. That's right, I was hauling down twenty-five bucks a night. And after I was done being MC, I had to DJ and spin records for another five hours.

A comedian by the name of Dan Merriman got me my first real job. He came into Sparky's one week and just murdered. I thought, *That guy is funny. How can you get that funny? That is ridiculously funny*.

After a show, Dan came over to me and said, "You're funny." I couldn't believe it. That's like Pamela Anderson calling Barbara Bush hot. Hey, I'm from Texas, I love Barbara, but come on, she is not hot.

Then Dan said: "How would you like to come down and showcase at the Funny Bone?" I couldn't believe it twice. Showcasing is a tryout for comedians. It's like being in the school talent show, except if they like you, they give you a job.

A couple of weeks roll around and me and a buddy named Franky drive down to Shreveport, Louisiana. I go into the Funny Bone, do my ten minutes, and get a good laugh. The club owner asks, "Do you have thirty minutes?"

I lied and said yes so he said, "I'm going to book you." He gave me a date and said he was going to pay me four hundred dollars. I almost pissed myself. Four hundred dollars! Franky and I drove down to New Orleans to celebrate, by which I mean we got drunk. We went down to Bourbon Street, where I had never been before. We went into a bar and ate crawfish, which I had never eaten before. I was doing everything I had never done before.

There weren't many people in the place, so the bartender goes, "What are you guys doing down here?"

And of course I said, "I'm a professional comedian."

So he says, "Why don't you come back tonight and do a set?"

I said, "All right, I will."

So I show up that night with my bag full of props . . . and the place is packed. Now I realized that the bar is really long and narrow and the stage is at the far end and there is only one way out, the way I came in. I swear that place had grown three times since lunch.

The bartender says, "Hey, man, give me an intro."

"Intro? I don't have an intro."

"What's your name?"

I give him my name, and as I'm walking up to the stage and the bartender says, "Give it up for professional comedian Randy Carlington!" and I'm thinking, *Oh, shit*. It's never good when they screw up your name.

I get up on stage and nobody is listening. Nobody. My first two jokes go over like frog shit and I can feel my face get hot. My buddy Franky is sitting at the bar. Three minutes into my set, I see him get up and walk out.

When I got done, nobody said a word. Nobody had laughed. Not once. I was so embarrassed I just walked off the stage. I didn't even say thanks or good night. Nobody clapped. I didn't even say good-bye to the guy behind the bar who had suckered me into the worst night of comedy in the history of the world.

I go outside and Franky says, "Damn, man, that was awful."

Unfortunately, my act wasn't much better at the Funny Bone. I had seven minutes of material that I tried to stretch into thirty minutes and it basically became, "Who's drinking?"

I must have said that a hundred times. "Who's drinking? Who's drinking?"

At least the company was better. Every night, for six long miserable, humiliating nights, I would come off stage and Steve Harvey—yes, Steve Harvey, the future King of Comedy—would put his arm around me, chuckle, and say, "Everything's going to be all right. You're going to be all right." Then Steve would go on stage, and he would kill them. He would murder them. He would do so well they forgot I had ever been on.

At the end of the week, the club manager gave me my four hundred dollars, but I could tell just by the way he was writing the check he was disgusted. He said, "I don't know what you were doing but before you started comedy, but drive your ass to Texas and get that job back."

I drove from Shreveport all the way to Longview that night, which is six hours. The whole time I kept thinking: *He paid me four hundred dollars and I sucked. He paid me four hundred dollars and I totally sucked. I wonder how much money he would pay me if I was good.*

THE SANDWICH

Eventually, I put together a half-decent comedy act. Mostly, it involved wigs and stupid voices. It wasn't very funny, but I had one bit at the end of the show that always saved me: The Seduction of a Sandwich.

I'd pull out a sandwich in a plastic bag and put it on the stool. Then I'd play a tape recording of a woman's voice, which was supposed to be the sandwich. She'd say, "Hey, you."

"Who, me?"

"What's your name?"

"Rodney. What's your name?"

"Ham and cheese. Do you like ham and cheese?"

"Sure."

"Good, because you're cute."

"You don't look so bad yourself."

There'd be an awkward pause "You know, it's kind of getting hot in this Ziploc."

"What do you want me to do?"

"Take it off."

I'd look around like a pervert, and then I'd slide the sandwich out of the bag. She'd talk about how great it felt to be out of the Ziploc. The conversation would still be about sandwiches, but it would get sexier and sexier.

"Do you like white bread?"

"You can cut my crust off if you want."

We'd be having a little verbal sexual affair, and finally the she-sandwich would get all excited and yell: "Eat me!"

And I did. I ate the sandwich right there on stage. Then you'd hear a knock on the door. It was her husband. I'd spit the sandwich back into the Ziploc bag and it would be over. It may sound corny, but it killed every time. People would pee, they were laughing so hard. That bit saved me many a night.

EVERY STUPID THING
MEN DO

Every stupid thing men do begins with alcohol. It happens. That's life. Of course, stupid usually happens when I'm on the road, working, away from the influence of my wife and children. I bet you know how that is, too.

My wife called me one night in my motel room and said, "Your blue blocker sunglasses came in."

"What the hell you talking about, woman?"

"You also got a wicker table, a Chinese ice maker, and a ceramic Dalmatian."

I just hung my head. Not again. When will I learn that QVC and liquor do not go together? I still don't know why I bought that Chinese ice maker, but I know why I bought those blue blocker sunglasses. On the commercial, the old boy put them on and said, "I can see real clear through these." I thought, *I can use a pair of those right about now because there are eighteen doors in this Best Western motel room and they are moving all over the place. I've pissed myself twice, and I still can't find the bathroom.*

But stupid isn't the half of it when it comes to drinking, because some of the smartest things men do begin with alcohol, too. Weird, ain't it?

Some of the best decisions I've made in my life have been made while drinking. I was drinking when I met my wife. I was drinking when I wrote *Fred*. I was lying on the couch in the dark in an apartment in Little Rock, Arkansas, strumming my guitar, and I started singing:

**I once shot a man just for snoring, got out of bed and shot
  him dead.
Chica-doom, chica-doom.
His name was . . .**

. . . and I stopped because I couldn't think of a name. I reached over, took a sip of my beer, and sang:

**His name was . . . I don't know what his name was, I just
  called him Fred.
Fred's riding Fred, Fred's riding Fred. Fred's riding Fred.**

Let's call that Level One Drinking. Having a few beers, getting loosened up, having some fun.

Level Two Drinking

Level Two Drinking is when you start to add stupid. But fun stupid. Like the one time in my life I actually attended a cocktail party. There are a lot of parties on the road because most comedians are young, single, and bored. Mostly these parties involved sitting around a shithole motel room drinking beer.

But this party was classy. Little trays of food. Nice music. Mixed drinks with little umbrellas in them.

Somehow, four of us ended up playing cards in the bedroom closet. That's Level One. Then we decided to take it up a notch to Level Two. We called it "The Naked Sasquatch." We decided the next guy to lose three hands had to, without warning, run through the party, up a spiral staircase to a loft, back down again, and then back to the closet. You had to run like you were a sasquatch in the wild, like you were an insane animal frightened by civilization. And you had to be completely naked.

I don't care how much you've been drinking, you get real serious when you don't want to do something. It's not like telling people, "Hi, I'm Rodney, and I'm going to run naked now, so if you don't want to see some flopping look away." Imagine the shock. All of a sudden there's a naked guy running past the hors d'oeuvres.

I guarantee you see a hair on something the rest of the night, you are not just pulling it off and eating it anyway. Especially if it's cocktail weenies.

Level Three Drinking

Level Three is where it tends to get a little scary. I'll use a country bar as an example. Level Two is when you take your good friend Mark Gross, a fellow comedian who wears a suit on stage, to a country bar in Omaha, Nebraska, and make him ride the mechanical bull. And while he's up there, you start taking bets with the local cowboys on how long the fancy fella in the suit is going to stay on.

Level Three is when you start the night with a white wine

spritzer down at the Ramada and somehow end it cold, alone, and at a different type of country bar, one of them where you take your gas cap and get in free. Instead of the mechanical bull, they've got a mechanical sheep, and some old fella stands behind it with his pants down, big old smile on his face. You go in the bathroom and some guy's trying to sell you gum, cologne, and a Snickers bar that's not in the wrapper.

But hell, you're drunk, so you go ahead and take a bite out of that candy bar, and the first thought that goes through your head is, *When did they start putting corn in a Snickers?*

Level Four Drinking

You want to take it to Level Four Drinking, you go outside in the parking lot, steal a lawnmower, and drive it down to the liquor store. The cop doesn't think it's funny when you pull up next to him at the red light with thirteen people sitting on the back of that sonofabitch. He rolls down the window and says, "Boy, what in the hell do you think you're doing?"

"I'm mowing. What does it look like I'm doing? You got any Grey Poupon?"

Level Four Drinking is when you take it too far, and unfortunately, like most of you out there, at least the ones that aren't lying, I've been to Level Four a time or two. In the early days, people used to send shots of tequila up to the stage, and occasionally I'd have about seven too many. One night, I peed in a cup. Just whipped it out on stage and had at it.

You thinking what I'm thinking? "That sonofabitch drank it!"

Sorry, ladies and gentleman, that never happened. But I have gotten so drunk I took my pants off onstage. And my underwear. In my hometown of Tulsa, Oklahoma. In front of my mother-in-law. And all her friends from work. My wife has never let me hear the end of that one.

Level Five Drinking

That's relatively harmless for a Level Four Drinking incident. Level Fours are no laughing matter. You got no control in a Level Four; it can screw you for life. Especially when there is a casino around.

Hell, put a bottle of liquor and a casino together and you've got a Level Five emergency already in progress. I went to one of those Indian casinos, drank the firewater, lost enough to keep the whole tribe in moccasins for a year. I drove in with a Cadillac, walked away with two dollars and a beaver pelt. We may have stolen their land, but we're slowly giving it back one nickel at a time.

Casinos and drinking are like chocolate and potato chips. They're both great ideas, but they just don't go together. Problem is, it seems like they should. They got chocolate-covered peanuts, right? They're delicious, right? So why not chocolate-covered potato chips? So you take a handful of Pringles, dip them in some chocolate . . . and next thing you know you wake up passed out on the floor with a terrible stomachache and you have no idea where your pants are.

That happened to me in 1991. I had been driving a lot, doing a lot of stressful one-nighters. At this point, I was just making a living. If I ate at Denny's, it seemed like the Four Seasons. I'd order the Grand Slam Breakfast and feel like a movie star.

One night I went into a Biloxi casino, and I won twelve hundred dollars playing blackjack. A few days later I had some time off and most of that money stashed away in the glove box of my truck, so I decided to stop back in Biloxi at the same casino and take a crack at another twelve hundred dollars.

I thought, *It's all right, I'm only going to take in two hundred dollars*, which was the same amount I had taken in when I won that money. I even pulled the same shirt out of the dirty clothes pile in the back of my truck because I thought that'd bring me luck. I think you see where this story is headed.

Like most gamblers, I went in happy. Titties and gambling, those are two things that can make you happy just thinking about them. I skipped up to the door holding hands with an old lady from Kalamazoo, just grinning.

It was 7:00 P.M. when I started, and over a six-hour period I lost the two hundred dollars playing blackjack, just slow-played and lost it. Of course, I'd been drinking the whole six hours, which put me on about Level Four, so I decided to go back out to the truck and get another hundred dollars out of the glove box. I kept drinking and going back out to the truck and at some point I crossed over to Level Five and by the time I was done it was 5:00 A.M. and I had a hundred dollars in my pocket and not a single penny left in my glove box.

I went out and got in my truck. It was raining. I had a sunroof that I had put in myself. It leaked bad. When I say leaked, I mean you might as well have just had the windows down and the top sawed off, that's how wet you got.

So I am drunk in my truck, soaking wet, dirty, hungover (you know how you can be drunk and hungover at the same time? Yeah, I thought so), mad that I've lost all my money, still can't believe I split those eights. Now I've got three days off, I've got nowhere to stay, and I've got a hundred dollars.

I walk in a Waffle House and say, "Can you break a hundred-dollar bill?"

The man says, "Sure," so I walked over to a table, sit down and try to kill myself.

I'm not joking. I ate about twelve fried eggs with chili and onions and tomatoes. I ate hash browns eighteen different ways. I drank a pitcher of Waffle House coffee mixed with grease straight from the grill. It was almost as if I said, "I better eat now because this is it, I am never eating again."

I wake up the next morning in the back of my truck and it feels like an oven. I'm still wearing the old dirty shirt I haven't washed in I don't know how long. I have a headache, I'm broke, I'm dehydrated, and worst of all, I smell like a Waffle House.

I tried to run from it, but I couldn't get away. It was inside me. Like cancer. I was sweating that artificial butter-flavored grease they use on the Texas toast.

Redemption

There are only two ways to go after a bad night of drinking: back to the bar, which is the last place you ever want to find yourself, or to a Baptist revival, and if you ever get the chance to go to one of those . . . jump off a damn cliff. Make sure there are rocks at the bottom because you do not want to live through that shit. A Baptist revival is where they try to make you feel bad for everything you've done in your whole life, and they do a pretty good job of it, too.

I went to a Baptist revival. I'd been drinking, thought it might be fun. I was sitting in the back row, minding my own business—coloring. Preacher comes out and starts screaming, "If you don't get up and come forward today the Lord is through with you, the devil's got you, I'm not kidding."

I dropped my crayon, I was so scared.

"I said if you don't come forward the Lord is through with you, the devil's got you, I'm not kidding. You with the crayon and the cowboy hat. I see you. You got sin written all over you."

It was like the Lord reached out his hand, laid it on my underwear, and gave me an atomic wedgie. I got up crying, walked all the way up to the front, said, "I've been drinking, preacher."

"You tell it."

"I've been cussing."

"You tell it again."

"I had sexual union with a goat."

"You tell . . . what?"

"It was heterosexual."

"Now, son . . ."

"And consensual."

"Now, son . . ."

"But God help me, preacher, I'm not sure she was sixteen."

"Son, please, just shut up. There are some things even the Lord don't need to know."

It's not the walk up there that's so bad, it's the walk back. All those good church people looking at you, thinking, *You really did that, didn't you, you sick sonofabitch? I know that goat, she's a good girl, now you've ruined her.*

Don't get me wrong, I love the Lord. We're on good terms, as far as I know. But do not go to a Baptist revival drunk, because the Lord works in mysterious ways. And he's sneaky. He will embarrass the hell out of you.

$20

That redemption bit is from my comedy act, which doesn't mean it's not true. My act is an exaggeration of my real life. I've been wearing cowboy boots since I was three. Been drinking since about then, too. When I say in one of my songs, "I thank God that I've got balls, a pickup truck, my Texas drawl," I mean it. I really have those things, and I thank God for them. The rest of that song is bullshit, but those two lines are true.

As you know by now, I'm from Texas, and until I was twenty that's just about the only place I'd ever been. Then I got my first big comedy offer, a one-week gig at a club in Cincinnati, Ohio. It paid $350. My dad drove me an hour to the airport in Dallas, which is good because after I paid for my plane ticket I only had fifty-seven cents left to my name. Seriously, that's all the money I had in the world.

I really wanted to make my own way in comedy without depending on my dad, my mother, or anybody else. I could probably have talked to my mom, but you know how dads are.

They don't say much, and when they do, it often ain't pretty. It's often just the truth.

But I was so broke that day, and so scared because I'd never been anywhere before, that after forty-five minutes in the truck I finally got up the courage to say something to my dad. Unfortunately, I was too chickenshit to tell him how broke I really was. Instead, I said, "Dad, I only got twenty dollars to get me to Cincinnati. Can you loan me another twenty dollars? When I get there, I'll get an advance on my paycheck and send it back to you."

He looked over, patted me on the back and said, "Ah hell, son, twenty dollars will get you there."

I LIKE MY WOMEN LIKE
I LIKE MY CHICKEN

Women are complicated, but there are only two types of men: single men and married men. The difference between being single and being married isn't the thinking, it's the doing. Married men are thinking about what single men are doing. And married men know what single men are doing because before they were married, they were single, too. And they spend the rest of their life wishing they could get back there.

Of course, in my case, when I was single I was also short, broke, and basically homeless, three qualities that really attract women. Thank God I like big women.

I'm on record, I've said it, you know it:

I like my women like I like my chicken,
   With a little bit of fat on the end,
Not too much and not too little,
   Just enough to make me grin.

I like big women because they come prepared, biscuit in one pocket, gravy in the other. Fat girl with a side of gravy. That is a night you'll never forget.

Hey now, don't get offended. I'm not prejudiced. I'm not part of the problem. I support a woman's right to look any way she wants to look. She wants to be big, have at it, be happy. I'd rather spend time with a big, fat happy woman than a skinny bitch any day of the week.

I don't want women to look like runway models. Those skinny women have committed the ultimate sin: They've made their titties shrink up. Used to be delicious sno-cones, now they're half-melted ice cubes in the bottom of an empty whiskey glass. Still tasty, but not nearly enough. I'd definitely rather have a woman with too many lumps than a woman with too few.

All you men out there know what I'm talking about. We've all been in the bar at closing time, nobody left but you, the bartender, and three girls in the corner booth. Eventually the girls call you over. The fat one passed out fifteen minutes ago, and now she's stuck. With the help of the bartender and few more shots of Jack Daniel's you manage to get her out of the booth and into your truck, and by that time she is looking pretty damn good.

Like I said, it's not the fat girls that are the problem. I love a big juicy piece of white-meat chicken, big old drumstick cooked in lard and dripping juice. The worst you'll get off a fat girl is greasy. It's the old chicken that's been lying around on the counter for anybody to try that will give you the worms.

I picked up a piece of meat like that once. It was in Fort Walton Beach, Florida, in the late 1980s. She had curlers in her hair, a gap between her two front teeth you could drive a truck through, dip of snuff in her mouth, breath like a trash can dumpster that could kill you. She drove me thirty minutes out in the country in her Chevy Blazer. Did I mention that her legs and arms had never seen a razor?

Ten minutes later the night was over. I called for a cab and the operator asked me, "Where you at?"

I said, "I don't know."

He said, "What does she look like?"

"She's short, blond, got a big ass."

"She got a birthmark?"

"She's got an extra nipple looks like the state of Texas."

"Hell, I know where you are. Sit tight. I'll be there in a minute."

I think you know where all this is headed, so if you've got a mind to, you can start singing with me:

Now I got this burning sensation when I pee.
When standing in a public bathroom, people stop and take
**   a look at me.**

Now grab your partner's hands, look her lovingly in the eyes, and whisper in your most tender voice:

I got this burning sensation when I pee,
And I got a damn good feeling you're the one that gave it
**   to me.**
I've got creepy, crawly crabs crawling all up over me . . .

You know you can catch crabs from a toilet seat, don't you? They jump off the rim, swing themselves over on a hair. You can't convince your wife of that, though.

. . . them itchy little bastards, I just can't get them to
leave.

Come on now, ladies, don't be shy. And don't pretend you don't
know what I'm talking about either. Where do you think guys
get it? It's not from each other, I can tell you that.

THE PEANUT, THE NURSE, AND OTHER STORIES I'D RATHER MY WIFE FORGET

I've already said it twice, but I'll say it again. There is nothing wrong with going home with a fat girl. Hell, there's nothing wrong with marrying her. They're sweet. They're appreciative. I went home with a fat girl once a bunch of times. Back in junior college I went home with a forty-three-year-old nurse that must have been at least three women in one. I couldn't see very straight, I thought I was about to have my first orgy.

She might not have been a looker, but this old gal had heart. She cared about people. She gave me a penicillin shot before we did anything, which I thought was nice of her. Then she lay back in the bed, pulled down the comforter, and said, "Get at it." I screwed the hell out of that comforter.

Thirty minutes later she said, "Honey, I'm over here." I jumped on top of her. I couldn't even touch the mattress with either hand. I had to balance up there. She started patting me on the back like she was burping a baby. So I burped. She said, "You smell like bacon."

Ten minutes later, she said, "You're cute. You aren't anywhere near the hole, but you're cute."

Of course, I've been with other types of women, too. Like the kind that get you all riled up and say, "Pee on me."

"Woman, you are weird. Get up, get out, and take your nipple clips with you. I'm not wearing them anymore."

It takes a lot for a man to call a woman too weird for sex. Men have the sexual tolerance of a dinosaur. A man comes out of a public bathroom and there's a woman in a dark corner with her miniskirt pulled up saying, "Look, sailor, this peanut fits right here."

"What the . . . shit it does, don't it? What you drinking?"

I've run into that crazy-ass woman, too, the one that scares you a little bit, but you like it. I had a woman a long time ago whisper to me, "I'm going to stick my finger in your butt."

"No you're not."

She had big, long fingernails, painted fire-engine red. I could have been killed. Comedian found dead. Fingernail stuck in ass. Blood everywhere.

Of course, I'm married now. I can't even talk about that stuff anymore because I'll forget my wife's birthday, forget my car keys, forget to zip up my pants after taking a piss, but my wife will never forget. Anything. Ever.

Ten years from now, we'll be sitting around the living room, reading magazines (her) and watching television (me), and she'll say, "Do you still think about her?"

"What you talking about?"

"That women who wanted you to piss on her. You still think about her?"

"That was a joke, honey."

"She was in your book."

"She was in my act, too."

"A book's different. It's got words in it."

"The book's the same, baby. It's all bullshit. You shouldn't believe everything you read."

She'll go back to reading, I'll think the conversation is over, and then she'll say, "What about that fat girl?"

"What fat girl?"

"The one with the food in her pockets. Do you miss her?"

"Well, maybe the gravy. That was damn good gravy."

Silence again.

"Do you want me to stick my finger up your butt?"

"Hell no, woman. My god."

Finally, she'll put down her magazine and come to the point. "Rodney, do you ever think about cheating on me?"

I'll say no, but in my mind I'll be thinking, *only every damn day*. Because that's how men are. We think about sex all the time. We aren't going to act on it, but we're sure as hell going to think about it. And you women shouldn't condemn us for it. There are men, and there are women, and one of us had to be the horny ones because sex is how we make sure there are enough people in the world to mow my lawn.

THE BIG FELLA

Let's face it, life gets boring. Same old job, same old house, same old pussy. At least if you're married. If you're not married: same old job, same old apartment, same old hand.

That's why, eventually, you end up doing something stupid. You find a big naked guy blowup sex doll with a big dick on him, and you think, *Oh, man, this is going to be funny*. Afterward you realize there is no way it wasn't going to end badly.

I know, because it happened to me. One night the tour bus stopped at a truck stop, and right next to the truck stop was an adult bookstore. Our road manager, Gary, went in to eat at the truck stop, and my friend Barry Martin and I decided we'd get a sex doll and put it in Gary's bunk. We were in the adult bookstore, poking around, and we stumbled over a life-size blow-up doll with a big dick on it and everything. He was six feet tall and at least a foot long.

We bought that big fella, and instead of trying to take him out to the bus in the box, then blowing him up on the bus and taking the chance of getting caught, we decided to blow him up in the store. That way, if Gary had somehow gone to the bus while we were buying the thing (we'd been in there awhile just, you know, window shopping), we could get somebody to go out there and have him go buy some trucker sausage and pork rinds while we got that big guy in his bunk.

I got down on my hands and knees and put my mouth on that thing. No, not that part, but it was uncomfortably close to his ass. Just then two truckers walk in and see me blowing up this big fella on the floor of the adult bookstore.

One of them said, "Look at that sumbitch. He can't even wait to get it home."

I said, "No, no, this is a joke."

"Whatever, pervert."

It's bad when you're getting called a pervert by a three-toothed trucker coming in to use the jerk-off booth. And this wasn't a classy joint either. The booth was a cardboard refrig-erator box with a three-foot-high door cut into it. Instead of a video screen, you had to use a Viewmaster. It's not easy trying to hold that plastic box up to your eyes, click the switch to look at the next picture, and choke the chicken at the same time. Not that I'd know. I just read about it in *National Geographic*.

It takes a lot to inflate a dick, let me tell you. By the time I got that dude blown up, I was so dizzy and light-headed I could barely see. We tried to hide the doll under a towel so we could take it back to the bus. I got halfway across the parking lot, and the towel blew off. I stopped, turned around, thought better of it, kept running but not exactly toward the bus because the blow-up dude was blocking my view. I'm running around and around in a trucker parking lot holding a huge naked dude who is bigger than me.

We got on the bus and stuck the big guy in the bunk. Gary came back and he was surprised, etc., etc., and after the laugh-ter subsided, well, Gary took a special interest in that big fella.

He'd sleep with him all curled up in his arms, and sometimes we'd hear a low moaning sound . . .

Nah. Come on now, it didn't happen like that.

Of course, that's what everybody says. No matter how much sex he's getting with the big blow-up sex doll, there isn't a pervert on the planet who is going to admit it. He'll always say, "Oh him? He's just a joke."

And that's the problem because, if you've got a big blow-up sex doll, eventually you're going to be in an awkward situation. In fact, if you buy a big blow-up sex doll, I recommend going out and purchasing something else immediately. You don't want to die in a freak accident and have the police officer say to your wife, "We don't know what happened, ma'am, but we checked his credit card records, and last thing he bought was a sex doll." That can make things a bit awkward at the funeral.

My situation was more typical. One night, we were parked outside a venue getting ready to do a show. I was eating a sandwich and watching television, and the blow-up doll was standing up in the seat next to me. A radio guy walked onto the bus, saw us, and went, "Oh, shit. Sorry," and ran out.

It took about ten seconds, but it finally dawned on me what the hell he thought I was doing. He thought he'd walked in on me getting very friendly with a big naked blow-up dude.

I figured I only had one chance: confuse him. I ran after him and said, "Look, man, I don't know what you think you saw, but I swear, it was only sex."

I don't know if it worked or not, but I didn't want to take another chance. I got rid of Big Jim that night. Just gave him away to a bunch of nuns, or maybe they were cheerleaders, I can't remember.

I hope they enjoyed him as much as we did.

MARRIAGE

You know how marriage works. Even if you haven't been through it, you've heard it before. Man. Woman. Boot camp. Drill sergeant. Sexual conduct. Dereliction of duty. No sex. She breaks your will. Marriage. Sex. Sex. Sex. Cramp. Shit! Injured by flying shrapnel. It's like the war stories your grandfather used to tell, except you're the one that dies in the end.

Of course, women are the ones who want to get married. Because they're romantics. No matter how many times they look at you, they never see the reality. They think, *Oh, we'll get married and live in a big house and he'll work and I won't and he'll lose weight and stop burping all the time and it will be like Cinderella and Snow White and Julia Roberts all rolled into one.*

Dream on, gold digger. Dream on.

A man never plans to get married, he just gets worn down. You've been in a relationship so long you think, *Oh, what the hell, how much worse could it possibly be?*

You find out when she starts planning the wedding. Every day it's something different: What do you think about the invitations? The napkins? The dress? The cake? The neckties? The fingernail files? The panties?

"Woman, I don't care what you wear, just make sure there's beer and whiskey after the ceremony. Hold on. Did you say panties?"

At this point, you still don't know how badly you've screwed up. All you know is that there's a big party, everyone's coming, and somehow you're involved. You get there and people are shaking your hand like you've just won a seat in the Senate. Your buddies are going, "Holy shit, you did it, man, you did it. You got married!"

Then they leave
   and you are stuck
      with one woman
         for the rest of your life.

It's not the emotional commitment. A man can tell a woman he loves her. And he can even mean it, too. Of course, he can also be drunk and just want to get in her pants, but is there really anything wrong with that?

I didn't think so.

The problem with marriage isn't the emotional commitment, it's the physical commitment. It's the one pussy for the rest of your life. Feels the same, looks the same, feels the same, looks the same, smells the same (is that country flower?), looks the same, feels like Jell-O.

Don't get me wrong, I like Jell-O. But not the same flavor every time.

GOLF

Sorry about the short chapter. I was supposed to be working today, but I went out to play golf instead. I went to a new course, which is always exciting. On the third tee, I hit the ball way off to the right. I asked the guy I was playing with if that was a good place to be. He said, "It is if you need to take a shit." And I had to, so it worked out. I played the rest of the round with no socks.

THE REAL STORY

If you have kids, it's eventually going to happen: They're going to get curious and ask you how you met their mother. And you'll be tempted to lie and tell them some romantic bullshit, especially if it's your daughter, because she's a child, she's innocent, and you want to protect her from reality for as long as you can.

But it's coming, people. Reality is coming whether you want it to or not. So why not tell your kids the truth? Because here's how life really happens:

You see a blond sitting on a barstool. Not only is she gorgeous, she's smiling. She's got personality. She's laughing at your corny jokes so hard she has an asthma attack and has to be resuscitated in the parking lot. Seriously. That happened.

You talk to this girl for five minutes and, my god, she is the girl of your dreams. So you get frisky and tell her, "I'm going to get you pregnant and marry you," which is the worst pickup line of all time, but somehow it works. You don't get sex that night, but you get to snuggle, and you're so lonely and horny it's enough.

But you really want to get in her pants, so you come up with a plan. You fake a near-death experience. Bingo, her mothering instinct kicks in. Every woman wants to take care of a man; it makes her feel even more superior than she already feels. Besides, how can she leave you dying from Siberian Swooning Fever on the side of the road? So she invites you to her apartment for chicken noodle soup.

And you never leave. Ever. You got a good thing going, and you don't want to give her a way out. So you do not take a single step outside that apartment. Not for cigarettes. Not for milk. Not for clean underwear. You just wear them until they fall off.

Of course, now that you're in her apartment you realize a lot of guys wouldn't exactly call this woman a catch. She works at the Budget Rent-a-Car. She's got suspicious cream in her bathroom medicine cabinet. She doesn't own anything except a water bed, a sofa, and two console televisions stacked on top of each other. You flip the channels on the top television to find the picture; the television on the bottom has the sound. Remote control? Not even close. You have to use a pair of pliers to change the channel because the knobs are broken off.

A week later you tell her the truth: I'm not sick, and I'm not really the prince of Moravia. In fact, Moravia might not even be a real country. The truth is I have a minimum-wage job. I drive a broken-down truck. And I don't even live in this town. I have to leave tomorrow or I'm going to get fired.

It works. You finally have sex, and it's so good you tell her, "Screw it, quit your job and come with me on the road."

She calls you three hours later on her morning break and says, "I did it."

"Did what?"

"Quit my job."

Oh, shit.

But it's fun. You love her. You drink tequila together. Sure, she throws up a lot, but that's what fifteen shots of tequila will do to you. Two weeks later, you're taking a piss back at her apartment. You look down and see a white stick sitting on the sink. You come out of the bathroom holding the stick and say, "What does a blue line mean?"

That's when she starts to cry.

Then you start thinking, and you realize she hasn't been drinking tequila at all. She's been drinking Kool-Aid. And she hasn't been throwing up at night, like a normal drunk, she's been throwing up in the morning after brushing her teeth.

That's when you start to cry.

Six weeks later, exactly three months to the day after meeting her, you're getting married at the Jesus Center, which is a corrugated tin building that doubles as a free wedding chapel and a bingo parlor. You're looking at the justice of the peace as he's reading that wedding shit and you notice there's a John Deere riding lawnmower back behind him, inside the building, kind of off to the side.

And you can't look away. The whole time you are up there getting married you are looking at that riding lawnmower and you are thinking, *This is great. The whole marriage, the engagement, the wedding, it's all perfect. I love this woman, and I don't have any doubts about it.*

The best part is, your mother-in-law pays for the whole thing: the wedding dress, the minister, the wedding cake from Albertson's grocery store. But she draws the line at paying for the reception, and you don't have anything planned. So you invite everyone to a lounge bar attached to a motel down by the highway. All twenty-five guests say they can make it . . .

except your new wife, who is having one of her frequent bouts of morning sickness in the middle of the afternoon.

So you ditch her and get drunk. It's a social obligation. You haven't seen Uncle Moose in three months, the guy's got six kidneys, and by God, he needs to put them to use. You finally get around to picking her up from her mother's house at three in the morning. She's wrapped in a sheet, freezing cold, runny nose, shivering. She looks like hell. As you're walking her across the parking lot, she falls over. You look down and realize you've stepped on her sheet. Instead of helping her up, you start laughing. You start laughing because you are so happy and so drunk and so excited because you are going to get to have sex with this gorgeous woman, and this gorgeous woman only, for the rest of your life.

And if you think that sounds like fun, wait until the honeymoon.

THE WORLD'S SMARTEST
HONEYMOON

Listen up now, fellas, because I'm about to tell you how *not* to impress your wife on your honeymoon. This is important. We call this lowering her expectations. It's too late now, you're married, she's stuck with you, and you don't want her to spend the rest of her life thinking she's got a reliable man who is going to provide for her and think about her needs and show her a good time for the rest of her life.

Best way to crush that dream? Act like an asshole on your honeymoon. I know it works, because I did it. And, thank God, Terri stuck with me, and it's all been uphill from there.

So here's how to ruin a honeymoon in seven easy steps.

1. **Make sure you have to work.** I booked a two-week job in the Bahamas, which sounds great except I was only getting paid $250 a week to work every day for about six hours. This step will work even better if you schedule the honeymoon

around a four-day, all-day training seminar at the packing plant in Akron, Ohio.

2. **Get her pregnant.** She can't drink, can't smoke, doesn't want to be seen in her bathing suit at the pool, and if you're lucky like me she'll have horrible, debilitating morning sickness the entire time.

3. **If she's terrified of flying, make sure you have to fly over the ocean in a tiny, beat-up airplane with holes in the bottom.** You don't know what scared of flying is until you've sat in a Kenny Rogers' Roasters chicken restaurant in Fort Lauderdale, Florida, with your hysterical wife. Everyone in the place thought I'd been beating the poor woman. She spent twenty-three hours on the phone—the *pay* phone—calling everyone she knew and telling them good-bye, I've got to fly shit airlines to the Bahamas with my cheap-ass husband and I'm going to die in a fiery plane crash, it's been nice knowing you . . . yes, I'm married. I got married last week. He's a comedian. I know, I know. What can I say? I'm an idiot.

4. **Don't bring any money.** We were broke, and I only got paid at the end of the trip, so we had to share one meal ticket a day. Terri would go down for breakfast and stuff herself at the buffet. Then she'd steal food for both of us. Nothing sends a message like forcing your wife to steal food to survive on your honeymoon! Most of the time, we just ate cans of tuna and beans. Stinky food is perfect for a pregnant woman.

5. **Get diarrhea.** Somehow, I managed to throw this wildcard into the mix, but I don't necessary recommend it.

6. **Gamble away all your money.** Did I say I only got paid at the end of the trip? Oh, sorry, that was just the lie I told my sick, pregnant wife. Actually, I got an advance on the money and blew it all gambling every night after my show. Yes, really.

7. **Keep lying.** The last day we're there, I go up to the room and say, "Honey, I've got to tell you something. I've been getting advances on my check and going to the casino. I've lost all our money. I have twenty dollars left, and I just found out there's a departure fee. It costs fifteen dollars each to get off the island. I'm sorry, honey. I think I've got a gambling problem." That last sentence was the lie. The rest of it is true.

Now that you've gone and screwed up the whole trip and possibly thrown away the best thing that ever happened to you, it's time for the final stroke of brilliance: Let her save the day. That way she'll know right off she can't depend on you, and she'll get stuck doing the heavy lifting for the rest of her natural life—or at least until she wises up and dumps your sorry ass.

Here's how it worked for me:

Terri just looked at me in that hotel room and said, "Well, Rodney, I'm going home. Give me ten bucks and if I have to borrow five to get off the island, that's fine. I'm going home."

I said, "No, no. Let's go down to the casino. I'll gamble and win it back."

She said, "How about you give me ten bucks, you take your ten bucks, and we'll both go down to the casino." God love her, Terri is crazier than I am.

So we go down to the casino. I sit at the blackjack table, lose all my money in about thirty seconds, and immediately I'm like, "Give me your ten dollars."

Terri says, "No! I am not giving you my ten dollars. I'm going home. I've had enough of you. Obviously I've made a huge, huge error in judgment."

Terri's never been in a casino before, and I can see her eyes starting to pop out of her head, she's so overwhelmed. Either that, or it's hard to waddle between the slot machines with all that baby weight. I'm a man. It doesn't matter to me. All I know is I've got to get that money from Terri before she does something stupid.

We walk by the roulette table. Suddenly Terri stops and asks the wheel man how roulette works. He says, "You put your money on a number, I spin the wheel. The odds of winning are thirty-five to one."

She says, "I want to put ten dollars on red fourteen." She told me later she was thinking of her twin sister's little girl, her first niece, whose birthday is December 14.

I go bananas. I cannot believe I am married to this woman. I'm yelling, "Are you crazy? Roulette is a sucker's game. Nobody wins at roulette. You are the biggest idiot I've ever met in my life. You are wasting our last ten dollars. I can't believe you . . . you . . . you just hit your number!"

I still almost can't believe it, but that roulette wheel hit red fourteen and saved my marriage. Terri won $350. We got off the island. We fell back in love. I'm jumping around, kissing her on the cheek, kissing her on the lips, grabbing her titties, fondling her ass, yelling, "Holy shit. Holy mother of shit. You are a genius, honey. You are . . . you are the greatest woman I have ever met in my life. I am so happy that I married you."

MEET THE PRINCESS

Marriage teaches you a few things. Unfortunately, you have to be married first to learn them, and by then it's too late.

Marriage teaches you to never start a sentence with "You're just like your mother . . ."

Marriage teaches you to never start an excuse with "I only meant to have one beer, but . . ."

Marriage teaches you the size of the gift must be at least as large as the size of your last screw-up. I'm talking about the size of the price tag, not the item.

Marriage teaches you to never, ever, ever, ever, ever, ever buy clothes that are too big for your wife. If you ever find yourself saying, "Sorry, honey, I didn't know you were a medium, I thought you were a large . . ." just stop right there and slice your dick off with a cheese grater because you are never going to be using it with that woman again.

And finally, marriage teaches you that there is nothing worse than a woman starting a sentence with "We need to talk." We need to talk doesn't mean you're going to talk, it means you're going to sit and listen while she tells you everything you've been doing wrong.

Take it from a married man, if a woman says "We need to talk," start a fire in the middle of the living room, throw in every piece of clothing in her closet, and run like hell, because the consequences of that are a whole lot easier to deal with.

A husband will never start a sentence with "We need to talk" unless he's gone out and caught a disease while fishing. It happens. It's happened to me. Twice.

The problem with marriage is that every woman thinks she's a princess, and once you get married to her she's going to start telling you all about it. It's not just that you suddenly have to treat her like a princess. That's fine. The problem is that, apparently, princesses don't give blow jobs. That is the dirty little secret about marriage. You say, "I do" and she says, "I don't do that anymore. Or that. Or that. And don't even think about that."

Not that I'm complaining. All right, I am complaining, but I don't have a right to complain. My wife is gorgeous. She's a great mother. Smart. Funny. Nice person, too. If you met her, you'd love her. I married way over my head. Hell, most men do, that's the advantage of women being so much better than us. Most of the time, they really are princesses.

But what does reality matter to a woman? Your girlfriend's ass can be as big as a truck, and she may be the nicest person on the planet, but once you knock her up and marry her, chances are she's going to lose the nice and keep the ass.

It's not her fault, though, not really. It's ours. Because marriage is like swimming. You have no idea what it's going to be like until you jump in. That's when you find out it's cold, it's wet, it's full of sharks, and when shit gets too deep you can't even breathe.

And then you panic. You haven't made a bet with Jeff on this marriage thing, you've made a deal with God. This shit is for real. There's no going back.

So you suck it up and do the most macho thing you'll ever do: You start to think about someone else before you think of yourself. Next thing you know, you're in the drugstore with your wife buying hemorrhoid suppositories because she's too embarrassed to buy them for herself. Funny, she never mentioned hemorrhoids before you were married.

There are eight or nine people in line, and right when you get to the front you realize buying hemorrhoid medicine is a little embarrassing. You slide the suppositories on the counter, no problem, nobody seems to be looking, and then your wife pats you on the back and says in a loud voice, "Don't worry, honey. These are going to make you feel a whole lot better."

She sold you out, my friend.

But what are you going to do? She's your wife, not your buddy. You can't get her back, because if you try, she will remember it for the rest of your life. So you suck it up and take the pain.

Ladies and gentleman, meet the princess!

CHILDBIRTH IS BEAUTIFUL

People say getting married is the biggest change you will ever make in your life. Not true. Marriage just changes your social schedule. Having children changes your life.

You don't know what love is or ever was until your first baby is born. When you see your first child for the first time, you understand that life is different now. You're living for a greater purpose—to train this baby to support you in your old age. At that moment, you completely understand how much your parents love you, which is scary and cool and shitty all at the same time.

Of course, you don't know anger and frustration and the urge to murder until you've had children, too, but that's a different chapter. For now, let's just say that once you have a baby you understand just how much children and parents mean to each other.

And at the same time you don't understand anything. You're like, *Oh my god, we've got a baby and I am a complete screw-up and, oh, Lord, my wife, she isn't much better. What are we going to do now?* It's like being dropped on a beautiful tropical island, just you and wife and the munchkin, and watching the helicopter fly away. It is the scariest and greatest moment of your life.

Of course, it takes a hell of a long time to get there. First you've got the nine-month wait, which is God's way of getting a man used to not being such a selfish, immoral bastard. When a woman is pregnant, you've got to do all kinds of crazy shit for her. I came home after a show one night and asked my pregnant wife, "Honey, you need anything?"

"Mashed potatoes and gravy."

"Mashed potatoes and gravy? It's two in the morning."

"I need mashed potatoes and gravy. I'm pregnant."

The only place open at two in the morning in Tulsa, Oklahoma, is Hardee's. They tell me, "We don't have mashed potatoes and gravy. We're serving breakfast."

I say, "Look. My wife's pregnant and she's craving mashed potatoes and gravy. I've got to have mashed potatoes and gravy."

They made a whole vat, which took thirty minutes, and I had to buy the whole thing. By the time I got home, Terri was already asleep. It took me two hours to eat the whole tub of mashed potatoes and gravy. I was poor, I sure as hell wasn't going to waste them.

Once nine months is up, most men think the wait is over. Nope. My wife was late, as usual. Typical woman.

We tried walking. Sex. Driving on a bumpy road. Sex. Prunes. Jumping up and down. Sex. She finally went into labor while watching John Stamos in *Full House*. It lasted twenty-three days. Not *Full House* (it only seemed that way), the labor. We got to the hospital at 6:00 P.M. on a Friday. I was showered, eating a sandwich, thinking we'd be out of there in a couple of hours. When I finally got out of that hospital, I looked like Moses. Big old long beard, toenails that hadn't been clipped in a month, raving about the flood.

There's nothing worse than seeing your wife in labor. Okay, I guess labor is worse, but I'm a man, I don't have to worry about that. The best way I can describe labor is this: Imagine somebody coming in and shooting your wife with a shotgun in the stomach. The gangrene starts to set in and you're just sitting there saying, "It's okay, I'm here for you. I'm not doing a damn thing, but I'm here for you."

She squeezes your hand and says, "Aaaaahhh."

That's when you realize she's dying and you are not cut out for this, you aren't even cut out to be a father, what were you thinking? For about half a second you think, *If I run now* . . . but then, nah, you're already in it for life, buddy, there are not enough beers in the world to help you escape this one.

"Honey, are you all right?"

"Aahh-urgghhh."

"Nurse. Get in here. My wife's dying."

Three calls like that on the intercom and they gave me an IV drip filled with Jack Daniel's to settle my nerves. Worst thing about it? My mother-in-law was in the room with me the whole time. They should have given one of us an epidural from the waist up. I begged them; they wouldn't do it.

Somewhere around noon my first boy, Zach, finally arrived. He was . . . he was the most . . . When you see your baby for the first time, you lose the ability to even begin to describe that moment.

Thank God other people are there to screw up the moment for you. The nurse said, "Childbirth is beautiful, isn't it?" Bullshit. I just saw fifty-two hours of childbirth and it was a lot of things, but beautiful ain't one of them.

Then my mother-in-law said, "He looks just like you." He was bald and didn't have teeth. He didn't look like me, he looked like Grandpa. They clipped his cord and he pissed on everybody. He even acts like Grandpa!

I was embarrassed at first when he peed, but then I thought about it. If I had the choice between peeing in a sack and lying in that sack for nine months, or holding it until I could get out of that sack and piss all over a nurse . . . well, I know what choice I'd make, don't you?

BOWLING BALLS

Do you know the worst thing about watching your wife give birth? It's not the blood and the slime. It's not the screaming and the cursing. It's not even the hospital bill for eighty-three thousand dollars.

It's the raised expectations.

When your baby is born, and you're in the room, you see something you never wanted to see. You see a bowling ball come out of your wife's vagina. And it's smiling.

I looked at the doctor and said, "That goes back to normal, don't it?"

He said, "I'm not sure, but for your sake I hope so."

I was scared. Really. I mean, I could have stuck three cell-phones and a catcher's mitt up there. You don't want that pressure on you for the rest of your life. It'd be like putting your dick in a coffee can. The only thing that'd make her happy would be your foot, and I'm not talking about a toe, I'm talking about the whole thing. That'd bring new meaning to pussy-footing around, wouldn't it?

I had this horrible fantasy going around in my head. I'm on top, trying like hell, when I realize my wife isn't even paying attention. "You feel anything, honey?"

"Nope."

"How about now?"

"You using the whole leg?"

"All the way up to the knee."

"Why don't you try doing circles?"

"Circles! I'm already trying squares."

"I'm sorry, sweetie. It's not working for me. Just give me a copy of that *Cosmo* and tell me when you're done."

So I avoided sex for three months after my son was born. It wasn't easy, either, because my wife's boobs were bigger. It happens for about six months after childbirth; then they start to shrivel up and get a little saggy.

That has got to be the stupidest thing God has ever done right there. The baby doesn't care about the size of his mother's melons, but he gets the big ones. Poor Daddy, who cares a lot, lot, lot, is stuck with the half-deflated balloons.

FUN WITH THE PARENTS

They say if you want to know what your wife is going to look like and act like when she gets old, just look at her mother. I'm glad I didn't know that when I was younger, because I never would have married Terri. Every time I see Terri's father, I just give him a hug. Poor bastard. Then I look at his wife and start to gag. He says, "Hey, now, don't rub it in."

I shouldn't make fun of my mother-in-law. For one thing, it ruins Christmas. For another, I'd only spent about thirty-seven minutes with her before the day my son was born. Hell, I'd only known her daughter for five and a half months. She was pregnant, I felt sorry for her, now I'm stuck raising a Mexican kid. Nice boy, damn fine worker.

Actually, I'd known my wife for nine months and ten minutes by the time Zach was born. That's me. Overachiever.

It's been more than ten years now, but I've still got a strained relationship with my mother-in-law. Fifteen minutes with her, and I want to shoot myself in the ball sack. Instead, I go exploring. I got into her medicine cabinet one time. I was trying to find whatever it is she takes that makes her so damn crazy.

I couldn't find it. Instead, I found a couple of travel pillows. I pulled the sticker off the back of one of them, stuck it to the back of my neck, and lay down for a nap.

Turns out it was a Kotex, which apparently is the brand name of something called a sanitary napkin. Have you ever seen a sanitary napkin? It must be like shoving a bale of hay down your pants.

Needless to say, it wasn't a pretty scene when my mother-in-law caught me napping on her Kotex. Mission accomplished: I'm not welcome at her house anymore.

Of course, my dad isn't any better. The older he gets, the weirder shit becomes. I don't like to admit it. I don't even like to talk about it. I don't even like writing about it right now, but . . .

I saw my dad's nuts.

Once.

It was Christmas. We were all sitting on the back porch, watching the kids run around, and Dad came out with a big bowl of green bean casserole. He sat down in a lawn chair and about a minute later my wife started gagging. I raced over to give her the Heimlich, looked over her shoulder, saw what she'd just seen, and I started gagging, too.

I don't know about you, but when I've got a nut hanging, I know it. I feel the wind, I push it in. Dad's over fifty, though, he may have lost some feeling down there. It took fourteen minutes of CPR on my gagging wife before Dad reached over and tucked his nut back into his shorts. Unfortunately, his other nut rolled out the other side and that's the moment, that second right there, when I got scarred for life.

SPLITTING THE HAMBURGER

Poverty's not that bad. No, I'm serious. Poverty's not that bad.

When you're young.

When you're young, you can do almost anything. When I was young, I ate nothing but cans of cold soup . . . for three straight years. I didn't even have enough money to drink enough beer to get drunk enough to pick up ugly women in bars.

When I got my first apartment, I was so poor I couldn't afford electricity. My friends would come over and I'd give them food and beer out of a cooler because I didn't have a refrigerator.

They'd say, "Turn on the television, Rodney."

"I don't have any electricity."

"So?"

"If I could afford a television, don't you think I'd have the electricity turned on?"

"Well, at least put on the lights. I can't see the cheese dip for my nachos."

"Lights run on electricity. No electricity, no lights."

They'd pop a beer and think about that and say, "Well, at least turn on the air-conditioning."

"No air-conditioning."

"How about that fan over there?"

There was something about no electricity they just couldn't understand.

What did I care? I was on the road fifty weeks a year. Most nights I slept in my truck. I would stack my stuff in the passenger seat and I'd sleep leaning against it. Then I got a camper shell and slept in the bed of the truck on some blankets.

Then it got even better. One night I drove in late to Longview and pulled into the apartment complex. There, shining in the headlights of the truck, was a twin mattress lying against a dumpster. I eyed the dimensions, and I got excited. I jumped out and sure enough that mattress fit right in the back of my truck, perfectly snug between the wheel wells. I went to Wal-Mart the next day and bought a new sheet and I slept on that mattress for two years. Finding that mattress was like Christmas and my birthday and hooking up with a pretty girl for the first time all rolled into one.

Then, suddenly, in the space of about three weeks, I had both a wife and a kid on the way. And I was still poor. When my son was born I didn't have twenty dollars in my pocket. I left the hospital the afternoon of Zach's birth, drove four hours to Fort Smith, Arkansas, did a show for seven people for two hundred dollars, and drove home. I didn't get a day off. There are no days off when you don't have any money.

We raised Zach on the road. His favorite toys were the wall-unit air-conditioners. He learned to walk in a Holiday Inn parking lot. We ate Thanksgiving dinner at Cracker Barrel. Twice. We gave thanks that at least it wasn't Denny's.

And you know what? It was still fun. It was like raising a kid in the circus.

I remember our first week on the road as a family. Terri was driving, I was lying on the floor of the used minivan I'd just traded my truck for, holding Zach on my chest. I could feel his warmth even though I was mostly asleep. I felt the van stop for gas, and then I felt Zach peeing all over me. It was coming out of the side of the diaper, getting all over my shirt. What could I do? I couldn't get mad. Hell, I'd done it to Terri the week before.

A few months later, we stopped at Whataburger, which is a fast-food restaurant. We pulled out the ashtray, which held all the money we had in the minivan, which was all the money we had in the world. We might have had some change hidden under the couch at home, but that was it.

We took the ashtray into the restaurant. I dump the change, candy wrappers, and ashtray lint on the counter and say, "What can we get with this?"

They count the change. Twice. Finally they say, "One cheeseburger, a regular fries, and two waters."

"All right, then, we'll have that."

We get back to the minivan, and I tear the hamburger in half. Terri looks at her half and says, "I think you got more than me."

So we start measuring halves. Then Terri starts dropping onions. I say, "You're dropping onions. Pick them up and throw them back on the hamburger. Don't be wasting food now. You've already got the bigger half."

"Shut up. You've got more onions than me."

We were serious. It was almost like we were arguing, but we weren't mad, we were laughing. You just got to laugh when you're so poor you're fighting over fried onions that have fallen on the floorboard of your car.

I call those splitting-the-hamburger moments. They don't mean much at the time, but later they come to mean something special, how you stuck together when the going was shitty, or how you could still have fun together even when times were tough.

Hell, I don't know what they mean. I don't know what anything means. I just remember sitting in that Whataburger parking lot, eating half a hamburger and drinking a cup of water, and thinking, *Everything is good. Everything is good, and it is just going to get better.*

SHOPPING

Ihate shopping, especially for clothes. I hate shopping for clothes so much I'd go naked if they'd let me.

But they won't, so I like to buy the first thing I see and get out as quickly as possible. I went to a garage sale once and found an old pair of underwear hanging on a clothesline. They were stiff as a board and mildewed down the middle. It looked like they had gotten moist in 1985 and never really got dry. The skid marks were up to the waistband. I really needed some new underwear, though. I was using Scotch tape to hold together the crotch of my current pair, and they were starting to give me blisters.

I asked the old woman in the lawn chair how much she wanted for them. Turns out they weren't even part of the garage sale. They were her husband's favorite pair and after he died of chronic diarrhea she didn't have the heart to take them down. Now they were stuck to the clothesline. If I could pull them off, they were mine, no charge.

Like any man, I love a bargain. I got out my crowbar, tore

those BVDs off the line. It's been ten years, and I'm still wearing them right now.

All right, that ain't true. The truth is that since the invention of the Wal-Mart SuperCenter, it's just as easy to buy a new pair of underwear as it is to wash them. The Wal-Mart SuperCenter, by god, is a man's shopping center. You can have your hair cut, get your taxes done, buy you some Toughskins jeans at bargain prices. Full-service bank. Cheap tattoos. They ought to put a titty bar in there, is what they ought to do. Take out the snack bar, put in some titty dancers. Suddenly, even the nacho cheese hot dogs are starting to look good.

"Excuse me, ma'am. I'll take a corn dog and a table dance. I'm going to do some shopping, but not before I see some nipples."

Of course, Wal-Mart's going to have to upgrade the quality of their employees for this idea to work. Nobody, and I mean nobody, wants to see titty dancers that look like that greeter fella. You know him, the guy standing right inside the door that goes, "Hey, you need a buggy?" He's got one eye looking off to the left, one eye rolled back into his head, you're not real sure who the hell he's talking to.

Lady greeter in a wheelchair came up to me the other day, "You need a buggy?"

"I got a better idea. I'll just push you around. You hold my shit."

You don't ever need a buggy when you go into Wal-Mart, do you? You're a man, you're there for one thing and one thing only. It's a quick in-and-out trip. The whole deal is like the first time you have sex, even down to the fact that you get two minutes into it you go, "Shit," because you just realized this isn't just a casual thing. There are strings attached. You go into a relationship for the sex, you end up with the bitching and the serious talking, too. You go into Wal-Mart for a bottle of body hair remover, you leave with eight hundred dollars' worth of shit you don't need.

Best thing about Wal-Mart, though, is the dress code. There isn't one! That's about the only place in Tulsa you can go in butt naked with a pair of flip-flops on and nobody pays any attention to you.

"Hey, Rodney, how you . . . Oh, Lord, what you wearing a belt for? You're nekkid."

"Well, Frannie, I just feel more comfortable this way. Knew I could come on down to Wal-Mart and be accepted for it. They'll take anyone here. You see that greeter fella? He ain't wearing pants either!"

And they'll take anything back at Wal-Mart. You can go back a year later and tell them, "These Pampers already got shit in them."

"We're real sorry about that. Run back there and get you another package." I had three kids, only had to buy one box of diapers.

Because Wal-Mart understands incentives. They've got tons of extra services to make shopping easier, but they're all aimed at women. For instance, Wal-Mart is the place to go if you want to whip your kids. There's always a little kid getting his ass whipped in there. There must be a little bell goes off in that damn place that only overweight women can hear. It's on dog frequency or something.

Ding—whip your kids.

You don't whip them, someone in there will whip them for you. Like that greeter fella. He's already got his belt most of the way off anyway: "You want me to whip him for you, ma'am? I'll whup the shit out of him."

Kids must be terrified of that place because that's where Momma takes them when they screw up. "Get in the truck, Breeanna, we're going to Wal-Mart. And while we're there,

I'm buying body hair remover and eight hundred dollars' worth of shit we don't need."

But I think Wal-Mart's got it all wrong. Why cater to women? Women already love to shop. They're going to come shopping anyway. I can't get my wife out of bed to go to work during the week (she's a princess), but I'll be damned if she's not up bright and early Saturday morning.

"Get up, Rodney, get ready. It's already six-thirty, and if we don't hurry up and get down to that garage sale all the good shit's going to be gone."

"Honey, it's a garage sale. There ain't no good shit."

Sure enough, we get there at seven-thirty, and it's all junk. But in her mind we're late, we missed the bargain of the century right here in old lady McGillicutty's driveway, so she's pissed. "I told you. I told you all the good shit would be gone. Now what's George going to wear to school this year?"

There is nothing rational about shopping and women. And it has nothing to do with need or money. Even poor women, not a penny to their name, love shopping. When we were first married, my wife loved to shop at the Cheapo Depot. They call it a store, but it's actually just the place where everybody brings the shit they couldn't sell at their garage sale. It's a warehouse full of the shit that people who buy shit wouldn't buy.

My wife used to embarrass the hell out of me in there. She'd hold up a Bahama Mama T-shirt like she was sizing up a prom dress. You know how women do it, drape the shirt over their tits in front of a mirror and sway back and forth. The damn shirt would have cigarette burns on the back. "I think if I tuck it in nobody will see these."

Then she'd want to try it on. That's when I'd lose it. "It's fifty cents, woman, just put it in the truck. If nothing else we'll use it as a rag."

Then she'd buy something and want to take it back. You

can't take it back, it's the Cheapo Depot, they're just trying to get rid of it. You'd think she'd been shopping at Dillard's.

Pick it up, look it over, size it, try it on, look it over, put it back. Repeat. Repeat. Repeat. Repeat.

Women have an amazing ability to not be bored by shopping. That's the difference between men and women. A man has to go shopping once a month, a man convinces himself all he ever does is shop. Five minutes of shopping and he gets bored and starts looking for something to do. I got so bored at a garage sale once I started jacking off behind the clothes rack. Unfortunately, I had to buy a jacket when I was through.

"That'll be fifty cents, Mister, that's nasty as hell."

My wife comes rushing up. "Can we get a discount? It's got a stain on it. That stain looks fresh, too."

MAN SHOPPING

It's never about the money. That's not why men hate shopping. I hear guys saying all the time, "My wife spends too much money shopping." That's horseshit. I never buy anything on credit, but on the other hand, I have never made a dollar that I didn't want to turn right around and spend. The problem is that women want to spend money on the wrong things.

First time I made a little money, my wife and I went out and looked at big-screen televisions. My wife said, "You know, Rodney, we don't need a big-screen TV. We're trying to save money" for this and that and some boring shit, I can't even remember the last part because I wasn't listening.

I said, "All right. I'd really like to have a big-screen TV, but we don't need one." But what my wife didn't understand was that they were giving us a real good deal, and that old television we had was just about to blow up, we were going to have to buy something anyway, it was just a matter of time, so I went back the next day and bought that big-screen. When she came home I had a bowl of popcorn on the coffee table and her favorite movie already in the DVD player.

Then I went out and test-drove a BMW. My wife said, "There's no way we can afford a BMW. We're sharing the minivan and that's the way it is."

A couple of days later I pulled up in the driveway with that BMW. My wife likes to tell this story because she says it's classic Rodney. It may be classic man behavior, too, I don't know, I'd like to get a second opinion on that.

I rolled up in that BMW and could tell my wife was furious. She said, "What are you doing, Rodney Carrington? What is that?"

"Do you like it?"

"Yeah, I like it, but we can't afford that."

"Well, it's for you, baby. I got it for you."

As my wife always reminds me, she never drove that car. Not once. Somehow, I always happened to have it out on the road when she needed it.

Then I bought the giant dicks.

I don't think anybody saw that one coming.

But I've got a life philosophy. My attitude has always been that if you want to be a star, you have to treat yourself like a star. When I think of myself as a bigger star, I become a better performer.

My friend Mark Gross, who is a great comedian, never bought into that idea. He'd say, "Yeah, let's do that, Rodney. Let's think if ourselves as big stars. But let's save some money, too."

I called him the first time I was headlining a comedy club. I had been on the road a long time, and I was excited. This was my big break. I was getting paid twelve hundred dollars for the week, which is more money than I had ever seen. I said, "I rented a Cadillac!"

Mark said, "You rented a Cadillac? What for?"

"To drive to the club and back to the hotel."

"How much was it?"

"Five hundred dollars."

"Are you an idiot? Don't piss your money away. You need to save your money."

I told him, "You got to treat yourself, Mark. We've been sleeping in cars. We've been eating cold soup out of rusted cans. You've got to treat yourself special when you can. Act like a star, become a star."

He said, "Yeah, yeah, enjoy the Cadillac, moron."

I called him a few years later and told him, "Hey, Mark, I bought two giant inflatable dicks." Mark had helped me write "Letter to My Penis" and the song was taking off.

He said, "Dicks? What for? You've already got a wife."

"For the show. They're going to go erect for the big finale."

"Dicks. Okay, I get it. That's kind of funny. How much were they?"

"Five thousand dollars apiece."

He almost had a stroke. "Rodney," he said, "don't buy them. Take the dicks back! Don't do it. You're an idiot."

I said, "Mark, how many times do I have to say it? You got to invest in yourself, and you got to invest in your show." But Mark thinks real loud, and I could practically hear this brain over the phone line saying, *Don't listen to that idiot, Mark, don't listen to him. He's gonna go broke. You just keep saving those nickels and one day you'll have enough to buy yourself that ant farm just like you always wanted.*

But I was right. Those penises were worth every penny I spent. Because penises work. People love the inflatable penises.

LUCKY

When I was in college, I took a modern dance class. It was me and twenty-six college girls, all wearing leotards. For the first twenty minutes, that was the best class I ever took.

Then we had to dance. The best way I can describe modern dance is . . . well, it is basically just how you move . . . it's just, kind of . . . there are no rules to modern dance. You have to move your body in the way that you feel it needs to move to a particular song. Or something like that.

It turned out to be real fun—the girls, the leotards—until I had to do a modern dance. I got up in front of the class and moved my body in the way the music made me feel. I really thought I was doing well, but I wasn't. The girls were snickering and laughing. Maybe it was my balls hanging over the seam in that damn leotard.

I didn't learn much about modern dance, but the class did give me a sense that, even in the adult world, it is okay to be funny. It is okay to have a good time. Once I realized those girls were laughing at me, I just went with it. I took it to stupid. Getting laughed at is freedom, as long as you don't take it too seriously.

Humor has always been like that for me. If I was in an embarrassing or a boring situation, I'd defuse it with humor. Like school, which somehow managed to be embarrassing and boring at the same time. So I would write "big hairy pussy" on a piece of paper and pass it back to my friend Marty Plyler in the middle of class. Then I would draw a picture. I was in seventh grade, I didn't know what I was drawing, it looked like a weasel exploded. I remember that picture falling on the ground and the teacher walking over and picking it up and going, "Is this funny to you, Mr. Carrington?"

"Yes, sir, it is."

I was sent to the principal's office. He took one look at that paper and said, "That's funny, but you can't make a living off dirty jokes."

Apparently, he was wrong.

When I first started writing comedy, I would sit down and pretend to write a letter to my old friend Marty Plyler. I figured if I could make pretend Marty laugh, everybody would laugh. I'd put stamps on the letters and mail them to myself. If I still thought they were funny when I opened them a week later, I'd try them in my act.

Dear Marty:

I finally met a girl. She's got a patch over one eye and a wooden foot. Her name is Lucky. I took her over to my friend's house the other night and got her drunk. We took her foot off and played hide the foot. She hopped around the house saying, "I'm going to kick your ass."

"Not until you find that foot, you ain't."

There's an advantage to dating a woman with a wooden foot. You get bored, you can always whittle. Last week, I tried it. Lucky said, "You seen my foot?"

"No, I haven't."

"You got my foot, don't you?"

I pulled it out from behind my back. "I put an extra toe on it."

A few days ago, I made a duck out of it. Now we don't call her Lucky. We call her Decoy.

I hope things are going well in Texas. Write to you soon.

Rodney

I told that story onstage and people started to laugh. Hard. That's when I discovered that the more honest I am, the harder people laugh. Not that I actually stole my girlfriend's foot (it was her hand, in case you were wondering). But getting drunk and stealing some poor girl's foot? That's really something I'd do. That's honest-to-God Rodney Carrington behavior.

FUN

Forget the romance and the respect and all the horseshit they feed you. The reason you get married to a person is because you have fun together. You say, "You're fun, I like you, you have a great vagina, let's get married." Then you get married, get her pregnant, and before you know it everything has changed.

Your single buddy, the one your wife hates because he always looks at her tits when he's talking to her and can't stay in a relationship more than five minutes, calls. "Let's go out and get some beer."

"I can't. My wife won't let me."

"What do you mean? You haven't even asked her."

"I can't ask her. That will make her mad."

"Why?"

"Because I'm supposed to know I can't go without even asking her."

"But it's all-you-can-eat wings night."

"Maybe next week."

But you both know you're not going next week. Or the week after. Or ever again. Instead, you're going to be at home, sitting on the couch with your wife, watching the Lifetime channel. And that's when you glance back into the bedroom and notice Fun is packing his bags.

"Where you going, Fun?"

"Nowhere. Just getting prepared in case something happens."

"Like what?"

"Don't worry about it, Rodney. Everything's going to be fine."

You wake up the next morning and Fun's gone. He didn't tell you where he was going. He didn't even leave a note. Now it's just you and her and the Lifetime channel and you really, really miss Fun. So you go looking for him, but he's not at any of the places you go anymore. He's not at the Sam's Club or the mall or the Applebee's. He's at the bar with the single guys, doing shots in a big sombrero with some stupid girl with big tits. And he doesn't recognize you anymore.

"Fun! It's me, Rodney!"

"Nice to see you, Roger."

"No, it's Rodney!"

"Whatever. Look, I've gotta go, Robert. This dick isn't going to suck itself."

You turn around and Fun's annoying half-brother Frustration is sitting on the other side of you. And he's smirking.

"Shut up, Frustration."

"I didn't say anything."

"I said shut up. I'm not listening to you."

But you end up leaving the bar anyway. Who can drink with that guy hanging around? You get in your car and sitting in the passenger seat is Responsibility. He's the mouthy one.

"Do you know what time it is?"

"Yes."

"Do you know tomorrow is your wife's birthday?"

"Yes."

"Did you get her a card?"

"Yes."

"Did you take the trash out this morning? Did you pay the light bill? Did you pick your underwear up off the kitchen floor?"

"Yes, yes, yes."

"You seem testy. Have you been drinking?"

"Yes, I have. Mostly because of you."

"You know what that means, right?"

"No."

"You'll have to deal with Guilt when you get home."

You get home and there's Guilt waiting in the doorway, smoking a cigarette. "Well, well, well, look who's finally home. Out looking for Fun, were ya?"

"Maybe."

"I thought I left you with Responsibility."

"I got him drunk and kicked him in the teeth. He's not coming back tonight."

"That's too bad, because while you were out looking for Fun, Tragedy stopped by."

"My mother-in-law?"

"No, you idiot, your girlfriend. Don't worry, I got rid of her."

"Where's my wife?"

"She's in there with her attorney."

"She want a divorce?"

"No, they're in the bedroom. Turns out she was looking for Fun, too."

It's going to happen. Maybe not the lawyer part, but Fun, Responsibility, Guilt, Tragedy, all the rest of it. Which is the primary reason if I had to do it all over again I'd marry my pickup truck. Doesn't shop at fancy stores, doesn't bitch about money, doesn't care if you stay out late and forget to call. A truck not only doesn't mind if you pick up a hooker, it'll give her a lift back to a sleazy motel. Buy a truck a new air filter every hundredth ride and it doesn't even need a wedding ring. Can you get that kind of deal from a woman? Not any woman you actually want to know.

But storming out of the house and running to your pickup truck isn't going to matter once Responsibility strikes. By then, there is no pickup truck. By then, you're storming out of the house and getting into your minivan.

NOW WE'RE COOKING

I never was much for book learning. Math? History? Chem-istry? It just never made sense to me. I'd sit in math class, looking at all those numbers, and think, *When in my life am I ever going to need to know any of this shit?*

Of course, I was wrong. I've been using that science every damn day.

Wait a second, no I haven't. I don't know the reason any-thing works, and I can still drive a car, eat a hamburger, and touch myself in the shower.

Hey now, don't starting getting all huffy, there's nothing wrong with a little self-pleasuring every now and then. Mas-turbating is natural. It relieves the tension. If God didn't want us to masturbate, he'd have made our arms shorter. That's why the Tyrannosaurus was such an angry creature. He had the arms of a Barbie doll on the body of a Sherman tank. If some-one had just jacked his big ass off, he might have been a little more friendly.

So math and science were out. It made no sense to even try

to learn that bullshit. What made sense to me was homemaking. In homemaking, they teach you how to sew and cook, and I thought, *Out of all the stuff you're going to need to know in your life, out of everything they can teach you while you're sitting on your ass in this school building, sewing and cooking are probably the most important.* My mother was a homemaking teacher for many years and she encouraged me to get into the womanly arts. It turned out to be a good thing, because for a long time I was out there on my own without a pot to piss in. Fortunately, I knew how to make one out of tinfoil and yarn.

I took homemaking class when I was in ninth grade. I was the only guy in the class. It was me and twenty-six girls, which is about the greatest thing that can ever happen to a fifteen-year-old boy. It was even better than that modern dance class. We were wearing aprons, cooking and sewing, stitching and bitching, tasting each other's cookies.

All the other guys were in shop making birdhouses. Now when is that ever going to come in handy? How many birdhouses are you going to use in your life—maybe two? And you can buy them for five dollars apiece at the rummage sale, anyway.

Eating. Now that's important. A McDonald's Happy Meal may only cost four dollars, but you've got to eat four times a day. Every day. For the rest of your life. What is that, $18 million worth of French fries?

Wait a second, I think I just did math. I'll be damned.

Of course, none of the other guys in high school saw it my way. They were like, "What are you doing in homemaking, you puss? That class is for girls."

I said, "That's right. Homemaking class is full of girls." They still looked like they wanted to kick my ass, so I spelled it out for them. "That. Class. Is. Where. The. Girls. Are."

I walked into homemaking class the next year, and it was all boys. Those bastards ruined everything. But not before I learned how to survive. By the time I started my comedy career, I knew I needed to find something that I could eat on the road, while driving. Something that didn't need a spoon, didn't need a plate, didn't have to be heated or cooked in any way, and didn't cost too much.

I tested every food known to man, although I'm sure women know about a bunch of other food since they actually go down the aisles in the grocery store that don't contain soup, potato chips, or beer.

I tried chicken noodle soup. I tried chicken and vegetable soup. I tried minestrone and chunky beef and even clam chowder. I finally settled on Campbell's Chicken and Stars soup. For three years, I lived on cold Campbell's Chicken and Stars out of the can. I drank so much Chicken and Stars soup out of the can I was destined to become a star . . . or a chicken . . . or maybe a can.

When I wanted a sit-down meal, I'd break out the cereal. I had a bowl that I carried with me, and I used to keep milk in the back of my truck. One winter I was up in Cleveland and a bunch of other places where it was snowing and cold. I was driving and doing one-nighters and the milk would freeze in the back of my truck. It was instant refrigeration. I would stick the carton under the defroster on the passenger side and defrost just enough milk for a bowl of cereal. Then I would stick it back in the truck bed and it would freeze up again. My homemaking teacher would have been proud.

Of course, I'm past the point of eating soup out of the can. Now I've got a wife. Most guys give up even pretending to cook as soon as they find a wife. That's one of the perks of marriage. For most men, cooking is grilling burgers or maybe, if they're ambitious, throwing a bunch of meat into a crock pot. A man's idea of serving a fancy, stay-at-home dinner is ordering take-out ribs.

There's a person like that in my family: my wife. She can't cook her way out of a plastic grocery bag. That's the one and only reason she's lucky to have me, because I'm a good cook. And there is nothing more frustrating in the entire world than cooking for three young boys. Every night it's the same thing.

"Daddy, can I have some ketchup?"

"You don't like that much, do you?"

"No."

"You're going to drown it in ketchup, aren't you?"

"Yes."

"You didn't even try it, did you?"

"No."

"So how do you know you don't like it?"

"Cuz I don't."

"You don't like anything, do you?"

"I like cookies."

"You're an ungrateful son of a bitch, aren't you? Do you know how hard Daddy worked on this meal? Do you know how long I combed through the garbage to find the ingredients for these trash tacos?"

I only call them trash tacos because they've got a little bit of everything thrown in. They've got cubed chicken breast and onions, grilled in a saucepan. Then you add bell peppers, jalapeños, any other spices and peppery things hanging around your kitchen, and two types of beans: ranch beans and pinto beans. I was only planning to use one type of bean, but I was drunk as hell when I invented this recipe and had a little trouble reading the labels.

Trash tacos are good, but they aren't my best dish. My best dish is squash casserole. If the ladies from the neighborhood quit snubbing me and finally invite me over for potluck and stitch-n-bitch, and I can only bring one dish, it will definitely be squash casserole.

I'm going to share my recipe with you right now. If Betty Crocker tries to tell you she's seen it in a cookbook, that's bullshit, don't believe her, because this recipe is a Rodney Carrington original.

Rodney's Squash Casserole

Take a 9-by-13 glass casserole dish and line the bottom and sides with soft corn tortillas.

Skin ten yellow squash and cut them into cubes.

Cook the squash with onions until the whole mixture is soft.

Transfer the squash and onions to a bowl and mash them up with a potato masher.

Add green chiles, olives, and those little fried onions that come in a can. If you're feeling frisky, strain a can of corn and mix that in, too. Corn is optional.

Add one can of mushroom soup and stir the whole thing together.

Spread the mixture over the flour tortillas.

Put at least three cheeses on top. I like cheddar, Monterey Jack, and Mexican cheese, but go ahead, experiment, it's your casserole.

Sprinkle fried onions out of the can and a little pile of diced tomato chunks on top to make it pretty.

Bake at 350 degrees for twenty minutes, let it cool for ten minutes, and dig in. This squash casserole goes really well with a naked, big-boobed horny woman, a bucket of beer, and a football game on television. Of course, what doesn't?

BARNEY SONGS

Men get the wrong idea about marriage. A man thinks once he gets married, his wife is going to do whatever he wants. If he wants her to get naked on the ceiling fan with a bottle sticking out of her butt, he thinks she's going to do it. Of course, if she asked him to get up on that ceiling fan, he'd be out looking for another woman, but a man never thinks about that. It's all take and no give with a man. I'm sorry, fellas, that's the honest truth.

And I'm even more sorry to tell you that the ceiling fan fantasy—nope. It doesn't happen that way. Here's what actually happens: you get married, you have kids, by the time you get to bed at night you are so tired you can't even think about sex. Finally, you figure out your only chance is to have sex during the day. So you create a diversion. You get all the kids together in the living room, shove in a DVD—"Look, kids, it's Barney"— then while they're staring at the television you and the wife run back to the bedroom and slam the door. You're back there nekkid, trying to get into it, and all you can hear is Barney songs.

I love you, you love me, we're a happy family . . .
Hello, Mr. Nickabocker, boppity-bop.

I can't even watch Barney these days without getting a hard-on.

Finally you realize you need to do things to spice the marriage up. You know me, I went right out and bought my wife some new titties. Bigger ones. Buying your wife a new set of titties is like giving her a fishing pole for her birthday: You know you're going to be getting a lot more out of them than she is. That's not selfish, is it?

I don't care if it is or not. I've only got one word for you on the subject: invest. It's worth every nickel. The day my wife came home with my new friends was like Halloween and Christmas rolled into one. She went right to bed, she was still so knocked out from the surgery. I went in, sort of giggling, and started rubbing them. I pinched myself, laughed, then said to myself, "Shhh. Be quiet. You'll scare the titties." I was like a kid in a candy store. I wanted to touch and lick and taste everything.

But it didn't stop there. We'd be driving down the road, and I'd reach over and touch them. She'd say, "Stop it!" We'd get to dinner and I'd accidentally squeeze them. Three times. "Stop it!" After dinner, we're getting back in the car and, you guessed it, "Stop it! If you're going to be doing that, I don't want you to hold the door for me. Gentleman, my ass!"

"Damn, honey, I paid for them, I thought I was going to get to use them. If I had known it was going to be this much trouble, I'd have had the doctor put them on *me*."

We stop in at a convenience store for milk on the way home

and she grabs my dick over in the Slim Jim aisle. "Hey, what are you doing?"

"Now you see how it feels. You don't like it, do you?"

"I like it. Let's just wait until we get home."

I jump in the car and drive a hundred miles an hour back to the house. I screech into the garage, jump out of the car, and then I hear it.

I love you, you love me, we're a happy . . .

And I know it's not going to happen. I can't do it. It's just too much work, and I'm too tired. Instead of rushing into that nightmare, I melt into a pool of goo right there on the garage floor.

"Honey, I'm going to, umm, fix my screwdriver. I'll see you in three hours once you finally get the last boy in his pajamas."

And after all that, the new titties didn't take. Seriously. It wasn't just my rude behavior. They didn't feel good (to my wife, not to me), so she had them taken out. That was a sad day. It was like watching your two best friends move off to France. They say they're going to come back and visit, but you know they never are, and even if they do come back to Oklahoma they'll probably be such assholes you won't even want to spend time with them anymore.

So you think up other ideas. I came in after a few weeks on the road and said, "Put on something slutty, honey, we're going to dinner. I want to drink some whiskey and get in your britches." Yep, I really know how to talk to a woman. It's called keeping the romance alive.

We went to a Mexican restaurant. The place was packed with Chinese people. Okay, okay, it was all white people. You never see Mexicans eating at a Mexican restaurant, do you?

We sat on the deck. It was a beautiful night. The sun was setting, the mariachi band was playing, it was very romantic. I was eating a chimichanga. My wife was wearing a miniskirt and slowly she flashed me some leg and my god, she wasn't wearing panties! There is nothing sexier than your wife not wearing panties and showing it to you in public.

Or at least that's true with my wife, because she's discreet. She's not one of those women that flashes a worn-out catcher's mitt every time she drinks a strawberry daiquiri and five shots of tequila. That's not sexy, that's awful. I've got a song about it called "Don't Look Now, Momma's Got Her Boobs Out." You may have heard it:

Don't look now, momma's got her boobs out
Showing everybody in town.

My wife is actually a little uptight about public nudity. In fact, she's so against it that this whole scenario, with her not wearing panties and showing it to me . . . I made it up. What really happened is that I was wearing shorts with no underwear and I tried to show it to her.

I kind of maneuvered around until one of my balls fell out. Then I started clearing my throat and nodding down toward my lap. It took eighteen minutes, but finally she noticed . . . and then she started choking on her burrito. She looked like a cat trying to cough up a hairball.

"Good Lord, Rodney, put those away. You are making me sick."

I've got to admit, testicles are not the most attractive things in the world. Actually, they are the least attractive things in the world. They're horrible. Wrinkly. Hairy. It's like God got done making man, looked down, and saw that he had a little pile of leftover bits, and was too tired to do anything but just stick them on. You think he could have done us a favor and given us something classy like a Crown Royal bag. Nice smooth velvet, got your name written on it. You can keep your spare change in there. Now, that's a sack!

Needless to say, I didn't get any sex that night. The closest I came was a late-night session of Barney songs and a leftover fish taco.

I'M ON TOP OF THE WORLD

The worst thing about having kids isn't the lack of sex; it's having to discipline them. I tried to solve that problem by being on the road working all the time. I thought my wife would take care of the discipline while I was gone, but she didn't fall for it.

Most parents know that the best discipline is a hot iron. Just touch it to their back, preferably on cotton, not linen, and they won't bother you again. But I'm a softy, I can't do it. So I came up with another idea.

Whenever my boys start fighting, which is always, I make them put their arms around each other, look each other in the eye, and repeat the chorus to "I'm on Top of the World." My lawyer tells me I can't write down the lyrics without paying somebody, so suffice it to say that the reason that fruit loop is on top of the world is because he's in love, and it takes him a long time to get to that point. After my boys say all that bullshit about love, I make them compliment each other. Then they have to kiss. Of course, my middle boy is now starting to slip his brother some tongue—just to piss him off, of course—so I'm going to have to do something about that.

This punishment accomplishes two things: It brings the boys closer together, and it entertains the hell out of me.

The problem is that they've gotten too close. One day, my oldest boy smarted off to my wife. I couldn't make the boy repeat "I'm on Top of the World" to his mother, that would be too cruel, so I said, "Zach, I'm about to whip you."

My youngest boy, who was five, carrying a plastic Viking sword and wearing a Viking helmet with two big horns, cowboy boots, and nothing else—which oddly enough is what I normally wear around the house—said to me, "If you touch my older brother, I'm going to light your ass up."

I went to whip his older brother, and sure enough he lit my ass up. He hit me in the shin with the plastic sword, and I did what any parent would have done. I grabbed the nearest thing and hit him in the back of the head with a limp fish my wife was defrosting on the kitchen counter. Which scared me, because he went down real fast.

I said, "George! George! Are you all right, George!?"

He jumped up and said, "Ha! Got you, Dad," and ran off.

Editor's Note: This chapter is a joke. Neither Rodney Carrington nor anyone at Rodney's Chicken Shack, Rodney's Car Wash, or Rodney's Exotic Massage Parlor condones any form of violence against children. So if anyone asks, the fish was a sardine.

THE ONLY LESSON
IN THIS BOOK

I never set out to be a singing comedian. The music came out of boredom. About a year after starting out in comedy, I bought a guitar in a pawnshop in Columbus, Georgia. I practiced when I was bored, which was always. I learned three or four chords, and one night in Lincoln, Nebraska, I took that guitar on stage and I played a song. Not a funny song. Just a song. It was like I was six years old: "Hey, Mom, look, I know how to play 'Mary had a Little Lamb'!"

The crowd is going, "What the hell is he doing with that guitar? He plays like a six-year-old."

The second night the club owner said, "Hey, dumbass, if you're going to take that guitar on stage, you might want do something funny with it."

So I started writing little bitty song snippets. The first one was "My Grandpa."

Grandpa got his teeth knocked out in 1952
By a stray foul ball Joe DiMaggio hit, the count it was oh
    and two.
I can't remember what he said when the ball hit him in the
    lips,
He tried to cuss, he tried to swear, but all he said was
    something like this:
Nnnnooffffuunnshhiiiittttuunnnnnnnnnnnfff . . .

So that's the one piece of advice in this book. No matter how much you want that souvenir, do not try to catch a baseball with your mouth.

TRUCKER SAUSAGE

It all started in Charlotte, North Carolina. We were play-ing golf one afternoon—me, my best friend Barry Martin, his son Darby, and Macon Moy, who worked at the local radio station affiliate of Bob & Tom. We came to the eighteenth tee, and I said, "Let's play the last hole for a pickled pig foot."

They all go, "What?"

"The loser of this hole has to eat a pickled pig foot."

I hit my ball down the middle. We were laughing between shots, making pig noises, oink-oink, oink-oink. Darby's next and he hits one down the middle. Macon hits one down the middle. Then Barry tees up and sprays one off deep into the woods. We knew right then who was eating the foot.

We drove across town to find a pig foot. I was excited be-cause I wasn't eating the foot, but I was getting to pick it out. I walked into a convenience store and asked the lady behind the counter, "Ma'am, do you have any pig foot?"

She said, "Naw, but we got pig knuckle. It's got twice the meat on there, it's a real value."

"Well all right, we'll have one of those."

The pig knuckles were in a big jar of pink juice. I pulled the cap off and just the smell of it made me gag. I reached in there and I got the biggest, nastiest knuckle in the bunch and I took it out to Barry, who was waiting in the backseat of the car like a slutty prom date. I handed that knuckle back to him and he bit into it like an apple. You know how when you gag real hard your eyes start to water? And you know how when you laugh real hard, you pee a little? All of that happened at the same time. Barry started crying and Darby, who was sitting next to him, laughed so hard he peed. He admitted it, he soiled his trousers.

It all ended one night in Midland-Odessa, Texas, outside the Grand Brother's Honky Tonk. There were seven or eight guys sitting on the tour bus playing five-card draw poker for shots of Egg Beaters, whiskey, and mayonnaise. That stuff is horrible. It will make you vomit. Guaranteed. People were running out of the bus, throwing up in a trash sack, then running back for more. The cheapest form of entertainment is watching your buddy throw up, ain't it?

There was a big light outside the tour bus, hanging off the side of the building, and there were moths and bugs flying all around it. You could hear them whapping against the wall. After we ran out of mayonnaise and Egg Beaters, I told Darby, "Run out there and get one of those moths and bring it in here."

Darby runs out there, and he brings in something that I am not kidding you is as big as a bird. And ugly, too. Big old legs. Antennae. We stuck that monster under the kitchen glass, and the whole glass started moving around the table.

Everything got real quiet. For about five minutes. One of the guys finally said, "This is bullshit. I'm not playing."

I said, "Then you got to leave the bus. If you aren't playing, you can't be on the bus to see who eats it."

He goes, "Well now, hang on a minute," because there is something in all of us that would like to see somebody eat a bug.

Finally everybody agreed they were going to play. Poor Barry Martin lost that hand, and when he lost we all started laughing. We were laughing because, first, we were relieved as hell we weren't the one eating, and second, now we got to see some really nasty, sickening shit.

Just before Barry eats this bug, his son Darby goes, "Wait a minute. What if this is some sort of poisonous animal that could possibly kill him?"

You know how sympathetic guys are when they have been drinking. We were all yelling, "Eat it, you puss. We'll worry about that later."

Somebody said, "You going to need a knife and fork to eat that sonofabitch." And Barry did. He had to eat that bird-bug in pieces like a Twix bar.

THE LAST SUPPER

Eating a big old bug is nasty. I don't recommend it. But if you really want to go Fear Factor, here's a joke you might want to try.

We were outside Cattle Annie's in West Virginia, hanging out after the show, and it was our road manager Gary's birthday. I'd been drinking, so I got inspired. I said, "Barry, take Gary in there to Annie's and get him drunk. I'm going to mix up some dog food and put a bunch of chips around it and make it look like bean dip."

I was in the bus for an hour, mixing slices of cheese with Alpo dog food and heating it up in the microwave. The whole bus smelled like a kennel. There were about six or seven of us sitting out there on the bus (including some people from Copenhagen, my sponsor—got a good word in for the dip boys). We set some chips around that dog food, and I've got to admit it looked pretty good.

Gary comes out. He's drunk and he's hungry and those chips were sitting there real pretty around that bowl of dog food. He started eating chips and dog food like he was in a Mexican restaurant. That first bite didn't turn him off. He never even hesitated. He was wolfing those sonsofbitches down.

We were all laughing, listening to the radio, and I swear "Who Let the Dogs Out" came on. We all started singing, "Who let the dogs out, who, who, who, who, who." Gary was in a good mood. It was his birthday. He was drinking and eating chips and Alpo, and he was singing along louder than the rest of us, singing "Who Let the Dogs Out" while eating dog food.

We were crying. We were laughing so hard we were crying.

Finally, the bus cleared out and it was just me, Barry, and Gary. I was lying on the couch, Gary was sitting at the end by my feet, and he said, "I don't feel too good."

I looked at Barry, and said, "It was real nice of the club to bring out the bean dip and chips, wasn't it?"

Barry goes, "Yeah, it was nice."

And Gary goes, "Yeah, hell, I ate a lot of it, but it tasted like Alpo."

DRUNK IN HEAVEN

I joke about drunk driving. I tell the story, which is not true by the way, of being so drunk on Christmas I almost got run down by Rudolph. I could see his nose. It was in two places at once. I tried swerving. I tried flooring it. I even ran off the road once or twice. I couldn't ditch that damn reindeer. Eventually, I got tired and pulled over to the side of the road.

Rudolph turned out to be the police car that was chasing me, and those officers weren't playing when they pulled me over.

"Put your hands on the wheel."

"Boy, am I glad to see you, officer. I could have killed somebody."

"Get out of the car."

"I can't. I'm drunk. How about you hop in?"

My parole officer tells me that's not funny. Drunk driving is no laughing matter. I tell him if you had to spend Christmas with my mother-in-law you'd get drunk, too.

He tells me you could end up in jail for drunk driving. And they won't let you out whenever you want. Even if your mother-in-law comes for a visit. You're trapped.

I'm from Texas, too, which means hard-ass jail. There is no such thing as easy jail in Texas. Texas has the kind of jails where you get a cellmate named Brutus who makes you an offer you can't refuse: four cigarettes for a kiss, five to make it French. After three days you're able to haggle him down to two cigarettes for a hug.

And you don't even smoke!

Of course, it could be worse. You could swerve off the road, hit a tree, and spend the rest of eternity drunk.

Actually, that might not be so bad, especially if you're headed south. In fact, it's probably a good idea to be a little tipsy when you get to hell.

"Damn, boys, it's hot in here. You gonna lose some customers if you don't turn the air-conditioner up. Hey, bartender, you look red. I'm just kidding. I'll have a piña colada, on the rocks, and maybe it's just me but I think that guy over there is on fire. Hey, big fella, like those horns. What you got, a poker? Ouch. What you doing? Ouch. Hey, asshole, cut that out. Ouch. Shit. What is wrong with you? That shit is hot."

Dying drunk might work against you if you're headed the other way. It's not a good first impression when you show up at the Pearly Gates and just keep ringing the doorbell because you're so drunk you think that's funny.

God opens the door and he's in a bad mood. "You been drinking?"

"I had a couple on the way up."

"I'm going to have to give you a sobriety test. Name the twelve disciples."

"Matthew, Peter . . . Greg, Marsha, Cindy, Jan, Bobby."

God's not laughing.

"Ah hell, God, I know it's the Brady Bunch, just let me in. I ain't playing. I was in here before. I just had to get my ID out of the truck. They forgot to stamp my hand."

I don't know for sure, but I got a feeling that isn't going to work with God. I bet he's a lot sharper than the bouncer down at the Tasty Pig Nightclub.

Of course, it might be worth it to slip a bottle of bourbon in there with you. That is if heaven isn't full of bourbon fountains and beer rivers, which I'm convinced it is. After all, it may be heaven, but Lord knows you're still going to need something to take the edge off because all those people that pissed you off in life—they're going up, too.

That's not good for me, because a lot of people piss me off:

When I'm sitting on a toilet, in a house that I don't know,
Looking all around me, "Where'd the toilet paper go?"
Feeling real uneasy, feeling real uncertain,
Got to wipe me ass again with a plastic shower curtain.
It's those little things, those itty bitty things;
It's those little things like that that piss me off.

Hell, I get pissed off every time I take the truck out for a drive. Some guy cuts me off and I'm like, "You sonofabitch. I'm going to kick your . . . Jesus Christ, you're a big bastard. I just pulled up to say I screwed up back there. No need to take your seat belt off, now. I got money."

You get to heaven, you get your wings, you become an angel. You look over and there they are: the nosy neighbor, the bad driver, the bitchy waitress, your high-school girlfriend, foreigners. The guy next to you starts singing "Row, row, row your boat, row, row, row your boat, row, row, row your boat" and he just will not shut up.

He farts, he flaps his wings, you sonofabitch!

"That's it. I can't do it. I cannot take this for the rest of eternity. This isn't heaven, God, this is bullshit."

An angel looks over and says, "Hey, asshole, who told you this is heaven?"

BARRY MARTIN

Imet Barry Martin in St. Louis, Missouri, in the early 1990s. We were working the Funny Bone comedy club together. We did our show every night and then went back to the condo and listened to George Jones. We got along real well. It was almost like we had known each other for a long, long time, like maybe in a past life we were butterflies together.

Barry had been a schoolteacher before getting into comedy, so he was a few years older than I was. In fact, he was exactly three days younger than my dad. Barry always told my dad, "I hope I look as good as you do when I'm your age."

Is that funny? Only the first three hundred times you hear it. That's one reason Barry and I got along. We had the same sense of humor.

Barry Martin was a brother, a father figure, and a friend. He was always there. If ever there was a question about anything in life, he always seemed to have the answer. He was a wise old man. Not like those idiots that rode camels for eight months to see Jesus, more like the mysterious old Chinese guy that seems like a bum but is really a karate master.

Barry and I had a lot of the same values, especially how we treated people and what we thought about family. For both of us, family was the most important thing. Barry took his comedy seriously, which means he could laugh. I never saw Barry angry, never, not once in the fifteen years I worked with him. He couldn't get mad.

But he could get drunk. Boy, could Barry Martin get drunk. We had a hell of a time. When the two of us were together, we would egg each other on. The reason I'd occasionally get publicly naked, besides bourbon, was Barry daring me. We sang naked on the bar at Cracker's Comedy Club in Indianapolis, Indiana. We jumped naked off a cliff in West Palm Beach and tried to swim to Donald Trump's house. The first night back on the road after a break, I'd order a chocolate cake and a case of beer to Barry's hotel room. You can't eat chocolate cake and drink beer together. If you try, you're going to get sick.

One night, Barry took ten beers and a couple of Darvocet, which are strong painkillers. I told him you only need one, but Barry says, "Give me two. I'm twice as big as you are."

Soon Barry started slurring his words, and eventually he said, "Ine gonna goat ta bad." We all thought that was a good idea.

We stopped at a truck stop an hour later and I bought one of those giant turkey legs like they sell at Six Flags. I opened up Barry's bunk and woke him up enough to go "here" and handed the turkey leg to him.

He was so out of it he went, "Oh, thanks." He grabbed it, rolled over and fell back asleep.

He woke up the next morning with grease all over his face. He brought that big old turkey leg out and said, "Who put this turkey leg in the bunk with me?"

I said, "I gave that to you last night. You were hugging it like you were slow-dancing with the fat girl in the last dance of a long, long night. I think you might have even called it Irene."

He said, "Good Lord, I must have been out of it. Don't tell my wife."

Later we were in Boise, Idaho, at the nicest hotel in town. It was Barry's birthday, so the people at the front desk helped me get a cake. It said "Happy Sixtieth Birthday from your good buddy Glen Campbell." Of course, everybody in the hotel was amazed. They kept going, "I can't believe you know Glen Campbell."

Barry had to keep saying, "Hell no, I don't know Glen Campbell. I hate Glen Campbell."

Barry took the cake up to his hotel room . . . and couldn't get in the door. I had had a thousand helium balloons delivered to his room. He had to open his window and push some of the balloons out. He called me, laughing, saying, "You sonofabitch, I can't even move in here. I've been releasing balloons for an hour and a half."

But Barry wasn't just my buddy, he was a very talented comedian. He was a flat-out funny guy. Barry got a record deal with a small label in Nashville, then one with Capitol Records. He was drawing his own crowds.

Barry worked with me on my television pilot for Touchtone. He understood my voice better than anybody. He was excited about the television show, and I was excited about the television show, we were like little giggly girls in a cotton candy store. We kept pinching each other with excitement, followed, of course, by a good smack upside the head. Men don't like to be pinched.

We flew out to California to talk to Touchtone about the television show on a private Lear-24 jet. We took a meeting, which is what they call talking business in Hollywood, and then we flew up to Pebble Beach to play golf.

We flew to Pebble Beach on a private jet! That might not mean anything to Mick Jagger, but you couldn't steal that experience from me and Barry with a baseball bat. We couldn't believe it, two boys from nowhere. We kept saying, "Look at this bullshit. Look at how far we managed to take this bullshit."

I remember getting to Pebble Beach. We got off the plane and within an hour we were on the first tee at Spyglass and I hit that first drive like a sonofabitch, long and right down the middle, and it was great, man, I mean, it was unbelievable.

A few weeks later, Barry and I were sitting out behind the theater in Baton Rouge, Louisiana. We had gotten to the show four hours early, so we ate dinner with the crew. We were laughing and having a good time. We were all a big family by then, so used to being together. I broke out my guitar and shared a new melody with everybody.

Barry was sitting at the end of a long picnic table, and he had his boot cocked up. He looked at me and he said, "That's really a pretty melody. What are you going to do with it?"

I said, "I don't know. Maybe we can write a comedy song that starts out real slow and pretty and then goes haywire."

He said, "You'll figure something out."

He paused, and then Barry said, "You know, I don't care if I ever perform again. I enjoy it, but the opportunity to write on this television show and be a part of something special, that to me is as good as it gets."

And I said, "Yeah, it's going to be fun."

After the show I said, "You want to ride with me to the airport?" I was flying home to check on the new sod out at my ranch.

He says, "Nah, you tell that sod I'll see it on Thursday." I hugged him and said, "I love you," and he said, "I love you," and that night Barry died in his sleep at a hotel in Baton Rouge.

Barry's death changed everything. It changed every single

thing in my life. I would look at his name on my phone, and I would realize I couldn't call him. I kept thinking I could, but I couldn't. Not to be able to call him every morning . . . not to be able to share a laugh over the phone. Never to spend any more time with him. There is nothing to prepare you for that. Barry Martin was truly the greatest person I have ever known. And he was gone.

I'm going to sing a song now in honor of my best friend Barry Martin. The song uses the melody I played for Barry the last night of his life. I know you can't hear this song, but if you could just hum quietly to yourself while I sing, or maybe just set this book down for a minute and think about the people that are truly important to you, I'd appreciate it.

Angel Friend

You lift me up, each day, even though you've gone away.
Your spirit dances, in my mind, in my heart, and in my
    soul.
The life you lived, the love you left, the ones you touched,
    we won't forget.
You gave us strength, in time of need, my friend, my
    angel friend.

We shared good times through the years,
and in my heart and soul you're here;
With me.
My friend, my angel friend.

I hear you whisper, in the wind, piece by piece our hearts
    will mend;
The dreams you shared we'll carry on, here and now, and
    beyond.
The world will smile 'cause you were here. The gifts you
    brought we'll hold them dear.
I'll take you with me till we meet again. My friend, my
    angel friend.

We'll share good times from now on,
'Cause in my heart you'll live on;
With me.
My friend, my angel friend.

I miss my friend.

WIENERS

It's hard being on the road all the time. You stay away from your wife for forty weeks, you get to be one horny sonofabitch. In fact, I'm horny right now.

I used to call my wife from the road to find out what's going on. She'd tell me, "The kids are in bed. The Barney DVD is back in the box. I miss you. I need it."

"I need it, too, honey, but it don't reach that far."

I'd send it to her on a plane if I could, but I'm pretty sure that's not FAA regulation. Can you see a pecker sitting up there in first class, ball sack draped over the edge of the seat, smiling and kind of humming to himself, "I'm gonna get me some, I'm gonna get me some."

"Sir, would you like a sack of nuts?"

"No thanks. Already got one."

Not going to happen. So I bought my wife a fake wiener. I went shopping for it at Christy's Toy Box in Tulsa, Oklahoma. I was dressed in an overcoat, a fake beard, and a mustache. I thought, *If I'm going in with these perverts, I better look like one.*

So I went the next step and didn't wear anything underneath. I got to admit, it felt pretty nice. A little drafty, but nice.

"Can I help you, sir? You've been standing over that air-conditioning vent for thirty minutes."

"My wife needs a weeny."

"Unfortunately, I can see that. Everyone in the store can see that. Please button up your coat."

I should have left right then, but I didn't. Instead, I let him lead me to the Wall of Wiener. Black, white, red, gold. Big, little, straight, curved, smooth, square, covered in blisters and boils. I swear, one looked like a cactus. They must have had a hundred wieners hanging on that wall. It was awful.

"What do you think of that big one up there on top?"

"My god, I don't want to compete with that. If I wanted her to leave me, I'd buy her that."

There ought to be a law where they don't make fake wieners over four or five inches long. And that humming shit, it ought to be illegal, too. We can't compete. You can't put a motor in your weeny, I've asked the doctor, can't be done.

He pulled one off the shelf. "This one looks real and feels real. Touch it."

"I don't think so."

"It's a popular model."

"I'm not buying a car, jackass. I just need a wiener."

I finally decided on a hummer with a great big motor and took it up to the counter. Waited in line with all the other perverts, tried not to touch anything. "That'll be $57.18."

What! For $57.18, that better be some damn good weeny.

Of course, I didn't have enough money. Had to put the weeny back, go to an ATM down the block, come back, stand over the air-conditioning vent, feel the breeze, love the breeze, get the weeny, get in line, buy the weeny, stand over the air-conditioning vent. It was a whole lot worse than not having enough money for green beans at the grocery store, that's for sure.

You can't put a weeny on a charge card. They'll call you about that. "Hello, is this Rodney Carrington?"

"Yes."

"Did you buy a weeny yesterday at 2:16 A.M.?"

You don't want to get that call. Even worse, you don't want your ten year-old son to answer and pretend to be you. When you buy a weeny, you pay cash, burn the receipt, and take the back roads home. But I didn't know that at the time. I took the interstate. Got pulled over. Cop said, "Let me see your license, and, umm, what's in that sack?"

"I'm not sure, officer. I stole this truck."

Finally got the weeny home—only cost me five hundred dollars in bail money, which I put on the credit card, no shame in that—and the whole episode turned out to be a terrible idea. Not only does my wife no longer miss me when I'm gone, now I never even see her when I'm home.

She goes in the bedroom and it sounds like someone is trimming the hedges in there. "You all right, honey?"

"Yeah, but my neck hurts. I'll be out tomorrow."

Hum, hum, hum. Hum, hum, hum. There is some serious weed whacking going on in there. "Terri, honey . . . can I watch?"

She didn't come out for four days. It took her that long to run out of batteries.

BAD BIRTHDAY PRESENTS

Here's some advice: Don't buy your wife a birthday present she can enjoy by herself. Buy her a little French maid outfit. Buy her those condoms you see in truck stop bathrooms that are ribbed for her pleasure. Do not buy her a vibrator.

You think she's only going to use that vibrator on herself to turn you on, don't you? Dream on, sucker, dream on.

The problem with a vibrator isn't just that it replaces you; you also don't get any pleasure out of it. Sure, sure, you get the pleasure of seeing your wife happy, but what about me! That's why two years ago on my wife's birthday I got her a gift for me.

Fake titties.

Again.

The first ones didn't take, so the second time around I got the Velcro kind. They tend to be a little lopsided and scratchy, but I'm not complaining. They're bigger than two Cadillac Escalades parked side by side.

That's the great thing about women: They keep getting

more and more like pickup trucks. You can have all kinds of work done on them. Buff up the thighs, raise the back end, put on big headlights, even get a bitching sound system, but if you do that you still have to put up with your wife's bitching. In stereo.

Of course, it's not the women that are the problem. It's us men. If anyone needs plastic surgery, it's us. As soon as a woman drives us off the lot, our bumper falls off. We get a flat tire right around the middle. Our dipstick gets droopy, oil starts leaking, and we smell like gas.

I feel sorry for women. I especially feel sorry for my wife, so for her last birthday I decided to do some in-home cosmetic surgery on myself: I shaved a little heart in the hair above my pecker.

I was in a hotel in Wisconsin. It was snowing, I was in the bathtub just bored, bored, bored. I'd already stuffed my wiener between my legs to see what I look like with a pussy, but it made me horny and my wife was a thousand miles away. So I lathered up and tried to shave a heart. It's not easy. After forty-three minutes that heart ended up looking like a diseased liver, so I shaved off all the hair. I looked like a little kid with a big dick. It was wrong.

If you think a dick is ugly with hair on it, try taking the hair off. A hairless dick looks like a sea creature out of its shell. You don't know this until you're done shaving, but men have fat on both sides down there. I looked in the mirror and yelled: "I've got pussy lips."

I started trying to make a toupee out of the hair I'd just shaved off. "I'm sorry, little fella. I am so, so sorry."

Three days later, I arrived home for my wife's birthday. Unfortunately, by then I'd forgotten my little shaving accident and bought her a fishing pole, which she has been nice enough to let me use. Turns out she doesn't like fishing.

The next morning I got out of shower and my wife said, "What the hell did you do, Rodney?"

I looked down and saw the naked fella. "Oh, shit! I mean . . . ta-da."

She came over and felt around down there. "I like them. They're smooth."

I got cocky. "Oh, yeah, you like that? Well, then, helicopter, helicopter, helicopter."

Don't lie now when your wife asks you about this part. Because you've done the helicopter. We've all done the helicopter. You come out of the shower. It's a little longer from the heat. You're alone so you whip off the towel, look in the mirror, sway your hips and start to swing that dick: helicopter, helicopter, helicopter!

THE WHEEL OF HORNY

You remember when we discovered masturbation, fellas? We didn't get shit done that week, did we? That's all we did. We'd be thinking, *This feels great. How come nobody told me about this?* Then the damn thing would go off and nearly blow a hole in the wall.

Of course, Daddy always made you feel guilty. He'd say, "Don't go pulling on your pecker. You'll yank that sonofabitch off, end up like your sister. You know she used to be your brother. Now get in here and eat."

Masturbation goes away for a while, but once you been married for a decade it starts to come back. It just gets too tiresome to try to convince your wife to do it with you. There's a whole damn process you have to go through to get anything. You can't just show it to her. Ta-da! Helicopter, helicopter . . . ah hell, never mind.

After thirteen years of marriage, I don't even know what I'm waking up to. It's basically spin the big mood wheel.

"Happy, sad, happy, sad, happy . . . HORNY, HORNY,

yes, come on, HORNY. Bitchy, oh no, not bitchy again. I don't want bitchy."

Of course, it's rigged against you. Bitchy's half the wheel. Horny is the tiniest little sliver. Horny is like ten thousand dollars and the trip to Italy on *Wheel of Fortune*. Nobody ever lands there.

That's why I thank God for the porno movie. I'm on the road quite a bit, so I watch a lot of porno. Well, not a lot, just two or three minutes a night.

They need something for guys like me—$2.99, the short version. I'm paying $12.99 for an hour of material, and I don't even get to the second scene. The first scene is always some overweight girl with a 1970s haircut, a jailhouse tattoo on her ass, and body acne. It's like they're trying to help you out by easing you into this thing. But not me. That girl gets me every time.

Then I watch the second scene just for the hell of it. And of course it's always better.

"Damn it, I should have waited. She's got bigger titties. Oh, hell, here comes another one. They're twins! Holy shit, they're twins and . . . oh, my god, I have never seen that before. I cannot believe I got off to a big, pimply girl with two old guys."

CRAMP!

Everything is on videotape these days, isn't it? The prom. The championship baseball game. Little Johnny's first shit in a real toilet. Don't forget to zoom in on the bowl, now. We want to see the shape of those floaters!

Poor Suzy goes to blow out her birthday candles, gets too close, hair catches on fire, she's running around screaming, and some woman in the background is going, "You filming this? You filming this, Earl? It's a keeper."

My wife loves that video camera. We've got just about everything documented. Including sex. That's right, we made a homemade porno movie. I figured I'd watched the first twelve seconds of 193 porno movies, I was an expert. Nope. Porno is not as easy as it looks.

Have you ever seen yourself naked on a video? It's revolting. And the good-looking people aren't any better. My wife is gorgeous, but I got the camera too close and her ass looked like a big boneless ham with a tiny little bone trying to make its way back in there. My finger kept poking up from the bottom of the frame like a hyper guy in a movie theater.

Maybe it's best my face wasn't on camera, because when I'm getting after it my tongue comes out. When I'm really getting after it, those teeth come out and cover up my bottom lip. I start making motor noises, like I'm revving the engine and putting it into gear. I'd fall down if I wasn't wearing my cleats.

Finally, my wife says, "Rodney, quit practicing in front of the mirror. Let's get started already."

I set the camera down, carefully lined it up . . . and somehow managed to zoom in all the way. The only thing you could see was the bottom of my foot tightening up.

Of course, I had the sexy talk going, "You like that, honey? Oh yeah." Tighten up, relax. Tighten up, relax. "You know you want it. Oh yeah. That's a lot. Lot, lot, lot, lot, lot. Oh shit. Cramp!"

Then I farted.

"Sorry, honey."

"Damn, Rodney, that stinks. What you been eating, dog food?"

I farted again.

"That's it. Turn that camera off."

I farted one more time. It was awful. You fart once in a porno movie, that's a comedy. You fart twice, that's a tragedy. You fart three times, that's a documentary. I call mine "A Hot Woman and a Fat Dude Going at It After a Dinner of Nachos and Beans." You can check it out for yourself because somehow that videotape ended up on the damn Internet.

Because I put it there. You're welcome. It's been up two years and I've already got seven hits. Of course, I've been on seven times to check out how many hits we've had, so maybe hearing a grown man fart isn't as exciting as I think it is.

ADULT DISNEY WORLD

I've been talking about marriage like it's all sex, sex, sex, or more accurately trying, trying, trying to get sex. But it's not. There are kids involved, and they aren't just talking birth control pills that keep their numbers down by constantly walking in and asking for chocolate milk when you're trying to have an intimate moment with the wife.

Kids are work. You've got to care for them and love them. You've got to give them things, like guidance and respect and a good hard kick in the backside. And eventually, if you've got kids, there is one place you have to end up going: Disney World.

It's a real hoot, that Disney World. You spend three thousand dollars to get in, spend sixteen hours waiting in line, and ride three rides. One of the rides is It's a Small World.

It's a small world after all, it's a small world after all.

That is the worst ride in amusement park history. I'd like to find Walt Disney, dig his ass up, and kick him in the nuts, it's so bad. You wait thirteen hours and it's not even fun. It's not even close to fun. It's the same elves singing the same dumb song over and over again.

It's a small world after all, it's a small world after all.

You're in a boat with thirty sweaty, stinky people, you're turning corner after corner and seeing more and more elves and there is no way out. Finally, you just go, "Screw it, I'm swimming!" But you don't, do you? You just sit there and take it like a good daddy.

I've got an idea, Walt. Take a back corner somewhere, put two elves on a log doing something nasty, make Daddy happy.

You get through sixteen hours of that goody-goody shit, and it's not even over because you've still got a forty-mile walk back to the minivan. You're wearing a set of crooked Mickey Mouse ears, you've got a horrible sunburn, you're carrying an eighty-five-pound Winnie the Pooh you won nine hours ago at a softball throw, and you don't even know where you parked. The kids are all cotton-candied up, going bananas, and you just want to kill the whole family, dump them in the river, and head home.

You get in the parking lot tram, which is another fourteen-hour wait. The poor driver goes, "Where'd you park?"

"Just take us home."

"Where do you live?"

"Oklahoma, jackass. Start driving."

I've got an idea to make Disney World tolerable: adult-themed rides. Leave the wife and kids over at the Mad Hatter's Tea Cups and head on over to Father Land. They don't have the log ride in Father Land, they have the Big Old Pecker ride. It's a big pecker floating in the water, six guys inside. Nice and simple. Up Titty Mountain, down Titty Mountain, rub the nipple as you go by and then—BAM!—right down into a big old puss. Not a clean-shaven, Hitler-mustache, manicured puss, either. I hate those. It's a garden, ladies, let it grow. I'm talking about a 1970s, au naturel, Buckwheat on a bad hair day puss. I want to come over the top of Titty Mountain and know Daddy is going into something dirty.

"Yeehaw! Here we come."

BAM. FWOOMP.

"Shit, it's dark in here."

"Wet, too."

"Do you smell that?"

"Yeah, what is it?"

"It smells like . . . country flower."

NOW I KNOW
HOW NOAH FELT

Every wife has a weakness. Hates spiders. Drinks too much. Venereal disease. Eventually, you're going to think you understand that weakness, and you're going to get lazy. But as soon as you take it for granted, I guarantee that weakness is going to rear up and bite you in the ass.

With my wife, the weakness is fear of flying. And the ass it reared up to bite was the one I'd used to sit in those horrible Disney World rides for the past five days. I know my wife hates flying, but it's sixty-nine hours from Disney World to Oklahoma in the truck. There is no way I'm driving.

So my wife got up early on the appointed morning, took ten Valium, and went to the airport. My youngest, George, was still riding in the car seat, so it was like wrestling a big ball of rattlesnakes to get them into the car: kids, luggage, screaming kid, car seat, Disney souvenirs, kids again, because somehow one of them broke loose and is clutching the pinball machine in the hotel lobby.

We finally get on the airplane. We're sitting there, waiting to take off, and Terri's yelling at the kids, "Get in your seat. Sit down. Don't move. Moving makes turbulence for the plane." I did what any man would do: I ignored it and started reading *Cosmopolitan* magazine.

Suddenly, Terri got up. She started shuffling around and pulling stuff out of the overhead storage bins. I asked her what she was doing and she said, "I smell gas. This plane is going to crash. I'm getting off and taking the kids and you can fly on without us."

Isn't it funny how if a woman thinks a plane is going to crash, she gets off with the kids but is perfectly happy for you to stay on?

I said, "Don't do this, Terri. Stay on the plane. This is crazy. Everything is fine."

Fifty minutes later, we're in a rented Dodge Durango, pulling out of the airport parking garage. And I am as mad as I have ever been in my life. After an hour and a half of driving, the Valium kicks in and Terri is back to happy. I didn't say a word to her until we were halfway through Mississippi, which in case your geography is bad is three states away.

It took more than twenty-one hours to drive from Orlando to Tulsa, but I drove the whole way. My wife disputes that. She claims she drove the last two hours from McCallister to Tulsa, but I'm a man, I know the truth. Why does she want to take away my glory?

One good thing did come out of that trip: education. Now I know how Noah must have felt. I spent forty hours with my wife, and I was ready to kill somebody. That poor guy had to spend forty days!

And it didn't start off well for either of us. I would love to have been in the house the night Noah came home to give his wife the news.

"Honey, I just talked to God, and he wants me to build a big boat in the backyard."

"Hell, Noah, if you want a boat, just get a boat, quit making shit up."

So Noah spends a few years building a boat in the backyard, measuring the damn thing out with his arm, getting the stink eye from his wife every time she comes out to hang up the laundry.

Now he's got to catch two of everything. Have you ever tried to catch an antelope in a robe and sandals? Not so easy. Noah isn't a young man, either, he's an older gentleman. The Bible said he was 218 years old or something like that.

Let's say Noah did manage to catch an antelope. Then what? He'd be wrestling it, breathing hard, trying to look between its legs.

"Okay." Breathe, breathe, breathe. "Okay. Now I need a girl."

Noah was clearly a man great in his faith. He never questioned God. We, as people today, don't have that sort of faith. What would you do if God came to you right now and said, "Larry, you're the only one worthy, you and your wife. The rest of these people, I'm sick of them. I want you to build a boat, collect two of everything, and wait."

I know what you'd say. You'd say, "Is that you, Jerry? I know it's you, you sick sonofabitch. You can't fool me. Sure, I'm worthy, but my wife? You want to save her? Yeah, right!"

"No Larry, it's really me, God."

"God? That really you? Oh, shit. Sorry. I didn't recognize you. You shave the beard? Looks damn good. Oh, shit, sorry about the cussing."

"Just round up the animals, Larry."

"Animals? I'm sorry, God, I can't. I gotta work tomorrow. I used up my sick days when I lied about that hernia operation."

"Two of every animal, Larry. By next Thursday."

"Two of everything? That seems a little much. I mean, what's a lemur? Aren't they in Africa? That's a long way from Oklahoma."

Let's face it, if God had left it up to one of us, we would have a ferret, a couple of dogs, cats, rollie pollies . . . and a lizard.

But Noah did it. That dumb sonofabitch rounded up every animal but the unicorn. And his reward? He got to spend forty days and forty nights on a shit-filled boat with his nagging wife. Every time the poor bastard passed her, she muttered, "God told you to build a boat. God told you to build a boat . . . did God ever tell you to clip those toenails?"

"I told you, woman, I need the toenails to climb the walls and catch the possums."

Finally, after forty days and nights of living hell, the water recedes, the boat lands, and God gives Noah another task. He's got to repopulate the earth . . . with her.

You know at that point his faith gave out. You know he eventually had to go to his boys and say, "I'm sorry. I built the boat, I caught the animals, I put up with her for forty days. I can't do it anymore. I just can't. One of you is going to have go in there and do it with your mother, because I have had it.' "

JUST CALL ME

I spent two years of my life in Los Angeles filming my television show. It took an extra two years off my life, too. I'm glad that's over.

Los Angeles is the dirty clothes hamper for all the people you hated in high school. It really is. Being in Los Angeles is like being on the set of *Friends*. I'm so hip. I'm so insecure. I wear Abercrombie clothes. I'm rich but I act like I'm poor, or I'm poor but I spend all my money acting like I'm rich. Whatever.

Nobody calls you in Los Angeles. That's the thing that really got me. They have somebody else call you and say, "I've got Mr. Bigass calling for you. Please hold."

For the first four months, I'd say, "Well, when Mr. Bigass can call me himself, I'll talk to him," and hang up.

Then I started feeling bad, because I imagined the poor person that has to actually make these calls. It's like an Amish barn-raising to make a phone call in Los Angeles; the whole community gets involved. Mr. Bigass gives the message to his assistant, who gives the message to her assistant, who gives the message to his assistant, and on down the line until all the phone calls that need to be placed in the whole city finally funnel down to one pathetic person in a basement somewhere who has to say all day, "Please hold for Mr. Bigass. Please hold for Mr. Scrotumhair. Please hold for Ms. Whinypants. Please hold. Please hold. Please hold."

Seventeen people to make a phone call to ask you if you can come by the office tomorrow! This is why nothing ever gets done in Los Angeles.

I admit it, I bought it. For a while, I thought Mr. Bigass really was so busy he needed somebody to dial for him. Then I was actually in the office when Mr. Bigass needed to make a phone call.

What does he do? He starts playing with that little ball thing on his desk, the one where you pull the ball back, it hits the other balls and knocks the one on the other side up. When he gets the balls going, he pushes the intercom and says, "Sarah, can you get So-and-so on the phone, please?" Then he just watches those balls go back and forth.

That's when I realized that people who ask their assistants to make their phone calls aren't cool. They aren't important. They're the world's biggest pussies. They are like the scared little guy at the dance who tells his friend, "Hey, go over to that girl and tell her I want to dance with her. And if she says yes, tell her I've got a big dick. Maybe she'll want to have sex with me."

Yeah, right, that always works.

LIVING LA VIDA CRAZY

The first day I was in L.A., they told me I was going to be in a big parade at Disneyland. They put me in a sash with my name on it and I thought, *Oh, yeah, shit's starting up now, ain't it?*

I waited in a room with all these real famous people, like the Desperate Housewives. I was the only person in there with a sash on. I asked the makeup woman, "Why aren't they wearing sashes?"

She said, "They don't need sashes. People know who the hell they are."

I marched in the parade next to John Stamos. You'd have thought I was walking next to Elvis the way the ten- and twelve-year-old girls were screaming. I felt like the fifth wheel on a unicycle.

It was all downhill from there. I got into drinking. And bar fights. One night, I was on the tour bus with Mötley Crüe. We'd been drinking all night. When we stepped off the bus, I saw a big line of ants crawling over to a sticky old lollipop, so I got right down on my hands and knees and snorted them.

No, wait. That wasn't me. That was Ozzy Osbourne. I heard that story on *Behind the Music*.

What I actually did in Los Angeles was work and attend promo events for ABC. I'd walk down the press line in my tuxedo . . . and people would have no idea who I was. Me and Nick, the guy who played my best friend Barry Martin, were walking into a press line once and the security guard stopped us, told us to go around the photographers, this was for celebrities only.

"No, no, we have a show on ABC."

"No you don't."

"Yes we do."

"No you don't. You're just a couple of hicks from Oklahoma."

The guard had to get somebody to check on it before we could walk down the press line. We're halfway down the line and I overhear a lady photographer ask the woman next to her, "Who is he?"

"I don't know, but he's on television. Just take his picture."

When I was a little kid, I wore a girl swimsuit. It was summer camp for poor kids. They were passing out swimsuits, and they ran out. Four boys had to put on little red one-piece girl suits. I told my mother about it, thinking she'd buy me a suit of my own, but she just laughed. That's when I realized if I was ever going to get something in life, I was going to have to get it myself.

But my point is this: As a boy, you never feel comfortable in a girl swimsuit. The whole thing is just wrong. Stuff doesn't fit right. Straps keep sliding off your shoulders, making your nipple stick out. After a few days, you start worrying that the suit is making your butt look big.

That's how I felt in Hollywood. I felt like I had a big butt.

Hold on, that's not right. I felt like a grown man in a little-girl swimsuit. Things didn't fit. You can't just take an Oklahoma cowboy and put him in Hollywood. It just don't work.

Take the "glamorous" parties. I'd go to the Golden Globe after-party, and I saw everybody that was anybody. I'd see all these people that I'd been watching on television, like Jamie Foxx and Paris Hilton. They'd be just standing around. It's like going to a zoo and seeing animals you've seen on *National Geographic*. "Hey, look, it's a lion [George Clooney]. It's a llama [Jamie Foxx]. It's a hyena [Damon Wayans]. It's a hippopotamus [Paris Hilton]."

I was a possum. I was that zoo animal they stick in a dark little cage between the popular animals, like the kangaroo and the zebra. The people that even bother to stop just shrug their shoulders and say, "Possum? Barely sings, doesn't dance, doesn't get drunk and punch out photographers. What's the point?"

Not that I didn't have a few positive brushes with celebrity. I played golf with Patrick Warburton, the guy who played Puddy on *Seinfeld*. After a few holes, I introduced him to the dog food challenge. He ate some Alpo.

And the cast was great. Mack Davis played my father-in-law. Now Mack is a legendary songwriter. He wrote songs for everybody, including "In the Ghetto" and "Don't Cry, Daddy" for Elvis. The first time I met him, he got out a guitar and played "In the Ghetto." It was powerful.

When he was done, he turned to me and said, "What do you do, son?"

"I sing comedy numbers, sir."

He gave me the guitar and said, "Why don't you play me one of your songs?"

I played "Letter to My Penis." He said, "I didn't know a fella could make a living writing shit like that."

I said, "I didn't either, sir, but apparently you can go a long way with a lot of hard work and few funny songs about your pecker."

FISH BALLS

Ithought I was a big shit when I was living in California. Just stepping into that state makes your skin tanner and your teeth whiter. Even if you drive a 1978 Gremlin, California gives you the urge to cut off the top, roll down the windows, and flaunt it.

So I cut the top off my truck and flew my family out from Oklahoma to show myself off. I figured I'd take my wife to Rodeo Street to do some shopping, because, well, I like rodeos.

We got into one of those hired sedans. They're like taxis for rich people, which I was pretending to be. I though, *Hell yeah, I got a paycheck coming. We're going to do some serious damage, boy.*

The driver was a pompous ass. I said, "Take us to Rodeo Street."

He said, "It's Ro-day-o Drive."

"Whatever, assho-lay-o, let's just go."

We went into the Ralph Lauren shop. He is awful proud of his shit. He puts his name on everything. Why does Ralph

Lauren want his name next to my ass? Is he going to try to steal my underwear in the locker room?

"Whoa, cowboy, them's my undies. See, they've got my name on them."

"Those your skid marks, too?"

"My god. What did you do? Eat a chocolate factory?"

The first thing I saw in the Ralph Lauren store was a six-hundred-dollar sweater. I almost choked myself laughing.

The salesboy sidled up. "Do you like it? It's cashmere."

He jumped toward me, and it scared the shit out of me. I thought he was going to screw me. But he didn't.

I said, "It might be cashmere, but the price is bullshit." That scared him, because he thought I was going to screw him. But I didn't.

He just slapped me and called me a bitch. "Don't you make a scene with me, Mr. Rodney Carrington."

I said, "How do you know my name?"

"Because it says so on your sash."

"Shit. I can't believe I'm still wearing this thing. I was in a parade with the Desperate Housewives, and I must have forgotten to take it off." I didn't tell him that the parade was three months ago, and I'd had the sash washed and pressed three times.

I ended up buying my wife one shoe. I couldn't afford the other one.

Then we went to a restaurant a few blocks away. It was called Real Classy Place on Rodeo Street. I couldn't read the menu because it was written in fancy, so I asked the waiter, "What do you recommend?"

He said, "Ze fish balls."

You ever seen balls on a fish? Me either. They must be tiny. I said, "I'm going to have to eat a million of them bastards to get full."

The waiter rolled his eyes. "Sir, ze fish balls are little bits of fish rolled inside round, fried cornbread."

"Oh, they're hush puppies with fish in them. Why didn't you just say so? They any good?"

"Very."

"What do they taste like?"

"Chicken."

I was once in a restaurant in Amarillo, Texas, called The Big Texan. The guy in the booth behind me said, "Excuse me, waiter, these mountain oysters—what do they taste like?"

"Chicken."

"What are they?"

"Bull testicles."

"You bring me chicken."

I'm a country boy. I agree with that fella. If it tastes like chicken, then by God I want chicken. I don't want any surprises.

I don't even think they should be allowed to call it mountain oysters. Put it on the menu like it is—bull nuts. That way you won't order them by mistake, unless you are drunk and feeling adventurous. "Waiter, bring me a double order of those bull nuts. And leave the hair on 'em!"

But I wasn't in The Big Texan; I was in The Snooty Californian. I figured as a good Oklahoman it was my duty to make a scene, just for kicks and giggles.

"All right, waiter, I'm game. I'll take some of them fish nuts, and throw in a chicken dick while you're at it."

The waiter sniffed, "Very funny, Mr. Carrington."

I looked down. Shit, still wearing that sash.

A DAY AT THE ZOO

After the embarrassment of Rodeo Street, I thought I better take the kids out for some fun. Everybody kept telling us we needed to go the San Diego Zoo because it's the best zoo in the country. So we drove down there.

It sucked. The animals were all in cages, and the cages were too far away from each other. That gave me a bright idea. While they were putting in the Big Old Pecker Ride at Disney World, they could improve the zoo, too. But this job would be easy. All they had to do was throw all the animals in one cage and get it over with. It would be a battle royale.

"Where's the lemur?"

"Lion got him."

"Zebra?"

"Lion got him."

"Possum."

"Lion got him."

"Lion?"

"Eaten by the giraffe. I had no idea those things were so vicious."

If that's not enough for you, they could throw in a death row inmate. If he can run through the lion cage with a Slim Jim tucked up his ass, we convert his sentence to life in prison without parole. If he eats the Slim Jim, we give him a pack of cigarettes. Everybody wins!

California wasn't all bad. When they give you your own television show for ABC, you get perks. Free coffee. Paper clips. One of the best perks, though, is that they give you a guide and you get to the walk to the front of every line at Disneyland. That's because ABC and Disney are the same company. ABC owns Disney, or Disney owns ABC . . . hell, it doesn't matter. All that matters is that when you have an ABC television show you can go to Disneyland at the busiest time of the year and ride every ride in about three hours, which completely ruins it for you for the rest of your life. You will never be able to go back and stand in line. I have seen my last trip to Disneyland.

It was worth it, though, because that day at Disneyland my kids thought I was the greatest thing in the history of the world. For one shining moment, Daddy got ahead of microwavable peanut butter and jelly pizza pockets on the list of cool. The boys just kept saying, "Daddy, this is cool. You are cool."

We'd walk past everybody, and they'd all have eat-shit-and-die looks on their faces, like they were all thinking, *Where in the hell do you think you are going?* It was embarrassing, because I'm not a celebrity. I'm a normal guy from Oklahoma. I've spent all my life waiting in lines. I can sympathize with the misery of standing in the sun for five hours and seeing somebody with a fancy escort walk past me to the front of the line.

It's not like I'm Madonna. That would have meant something. I'm just Rodney from *Rodney*, the least-famous television show in the history of the world. You can't say to somebody,

"Well, I've got my own television show and this is just part of it," because nobody gives a crap.

So I faked it. I bought a wrench and a Mickey Mouse flashlight, pulled my jeans down to show some ass crack, and pretended I was going up there to fix the rides.

It was all a dream. Two years later the show is off the air, and we're at Sea World on a family vacation waiting an hour and a half to ride the river raft ride. I said to Terri, "Remember when we walked to the front of this line? Not only did we ride it, when we finished riding it we stayed in the boat and told them we were going around again, but before we did we wanted a hot dog, some Cracker Jacks, and a bottle of whiskey, and they said okay and, by God, we went around again."

Terri said, "How could I forget that, Rodney? You chugged the whole bottle and threw up in my purse."

Titties and beer,
Titties and beer,
Hunting two-legged deer,
Titties and beer,
Sometimes I thank God almighty
For titties and beer,
Big old titties and beer.

Just wanted to make sure you were still paying attention.

YOGA

I joined a gym while I was out in California. I don't like to work out. Take one look at me, and that's obvious. I just joined for the yoga.

Watching the yoga, that is. My god, those women are talented. There was one woman in that class that could have licked her own vagina. If she would have just listened to me.

"Get down there, baby! Come on, you can do it! You want me to put my foot on your back? I'm not wearing my cleats. You want me to get down there and do it for you? It looks delicious. I'll split it with you."

Doing yoga in a gym is almost as bad as watching Jane Fonda in the living room. Have you seen that video? Women bouncing around in leotards on the beach, stretching. Did I mention bouncing? You can't do those exercises with a hard-on. I tried like hell, can't be done. Same with yoga. You'll put someone's eye out if you're not careful; you better just hope it's not your own.

It took four weeks, but eventually I got tired of watching

and wandered over to the man part of the gym. They had an old boy named Roy who taught boxing. He told me, "You should take my boxing class, Rodney. You look thick. You look like you could whip the shit out of somebody." I'm not sure if Roy meant thick tough, thick fat, or thick stupid—although I suspect he probably meant the last one.

I said, "Roy, I've never had to fight a day in my life. I'm quick. Gone."

Now, I'm not the fighting type. Fighting hurts. I feel like something is about to happen and . . .

"Where's Rodney?"

"Don't know. Hiding, I guess."

Or I take my pants off. You want to avoid a fight, drop your drawers, because nobody wants to fight a naked guy. You can scare a big sonofabitch with a little pecker.

But Roy started calling me champ. Every time he'd see me, he'd say, "What's up, champ?" He started introducing me to people: "Meet the champ. This fella here's the champ."

I start thinking, *Maybe I am the champ. Maybe I am a bad-ass and I don't even know it.*

I start training: getting up in the morning, running, jumping rope, drinking raw eggs, throwing up. Eggs stay down a whole lot better if you cook them.

Eventually, it was time for my first fight. Against Roy. Now, Roy's a big tall dude, about six-four, like me. Just kidding. I'm about three feet tall.

Roy came out and he had on fancy boxing underwear; I had on my jeans and a bathrobe.

Roy was chiseled and cut; I was thick.

But I wasn't worried. I had on my big red puffy headgear and my big red boxing gloves and Roy didn't know it, but up underneath those gloves I had my middle knuckles up. I was about to frog the hell out of Roy.

We sparred for a little bit, just dancing around the ring like they do in the movies. Then Roy said, "Now I'm going to start hitting you."

I said something stupid like, "Bring it on, asshole."

And he did.

Roy hit me in the ear. It hurt. A lot. I was still trying to rub it and get the red down when Roy hit me in the nose—nine times. You know how when you get hit in the nose your eyes start to water and it looks like you're crying? That happened to me, except I really was crying. Roy hit me again and I peed a little. I'm pretty sure I shit my britches, too. I said, "That's it, Roy. I quit."

It's not the boxing I mind. It's the boxing back I don't like. I'm a sonofabitch on that heavy bag. I'd whip the shit out of some old boy with no arms. He wouldn't stand a chance against Big Rodsickle. I often fantasize about some big-mouth, no-arms sonofabitch popping off to me. He's leaning against the bar, drinking beer out of a bendee straw, playing video trivia with his foot. He starts getting mouthy and I say, "Oh, yeah, you mind if I River Dance with your wife?"

And then it's on, because River Dance is the only dancing you can do when you don't have any arms. That and half the hokey pokey.

"Put your right arm in. Oh, shit, sorry."

"Put your left arm in. Oh, shit. Umm . . . anybody want to do the Bunny Hop?"

THE L.A. DIET

I'm not much on exercising, but if I've got to do something (and I do, or I'll look like a sumo wrestler), I choose jogging. The thing I like about jogging is that it's casual. It's just you, the open road, and whoever's in the Texaco when you stop halfway through for a day-old jelly doughnut.

When I go jogging, I don't care how I look. I just reach into my drawer and pull out the warm-ups Grandma bought me for Christmas eight years ago. They're a little tight. Actually, they're a lot tight. When I'm wearing those warm-ups it looks like I've been kicked in the crotch by a buffalo. My nuts overlap the seam.

It's usually women you see like that. And not cute ones, either. I'm talking about the skinny, lanky-haired, pockmarked ones yelling at their kids down at the Laundromat. They've got camel lips hanging. It looks like they could smoke a cigarette or pick up an apple with that thing.

"Good Lord, woman! Here's twenty dollars, buy yourself some bigger pants, for God's sake. I'm trying to drink a Coke and eat corn nuts. You're making me sick."

Those women are probably thinking what I'm thinking when I put on those warm-ups: I am a sexy creature.

Actually, I'm thinking: *Who's going to see me?* It's not like I'll be jogging down a dark road, some kid will drive by, and his headlights will hit me just right. He'll swerve off the road, hit a tree, and say, "Shit, did you see that, Josey? That boy's nuts were overlapping the seam!"

First time I went jogging, I opened the door at 10:30 P.M. in my warm-ups and my boots. I'm in the front yard stretching and my wife says, "Where you going?"

"Jogging."

She fell down, she was laughing so hard. I thought, *To hell with you*, and I jogged off into the night. I passed a cemetery. It looked peaceful, so I jogged up in there. Shit. There were dead people everywhere. I heard some rustling in the leaves, my jog turned into a raging sprint back to the house. I hurtled a ten-foot fence, dodged some lawn chairs, it was the best workout I ever had.

And it only took ten minutes. I came busting through the door, my wife was still on the floor laughing, that's how long I was gone.

But that's Oklahoma. It's different in California. In California, they jog during the day. My friend Jennifer Aspen, who played my wife on television, convinced me to go jogging with her. I thought that was nice, so I did her a favor and bought some new warm-ups. Good thing, too, because we drove down to this reservoir in the middle of a big park and there were a thousand people running around in there.

As soon as I saw that I started having flashbacks to my high-school track days. Then I started having the dry heaves. Then I started thinking. Two stretches into my warm-up routine, I pretended to pull a hammy and had to be carried back to the car.

That was easy.

I decided instead I was going to lose weight on that California diet. That's when you eat nothing but salad and tofu. It works, too. That food is so nasty you don't even want to think about eating it. I ate half a bag of those Styrofoam peanuts you put in the box so your ceramic fish doesn't break before someone told me they weren't tofu. I couldn't tell the difference.

Of course, I couldn't keep up the diet. I'd go to a restaurant for lunch and order six Caesar salads with chicken. And hell, throw in a side of tofu, I'm on a diet.

Then I started outright cheating. I'd have a salad for dinner, then sneak off down to a place called Mr. Cecil's for ribs, corn, mashed potatoes, sweet tea, and a side of fried chicken. I'd tell myself it was just dessert.

Then I started getting other people involved. Someone would come to town, and I'd practically beg them to go to Morton's Steakhouse with me. Then I'd order three sirloins and pretend it was a special treat. My manager came to town once and I ordered twenty-eight lamb chops. I'm not playing. I only ate twenty-seven of them, though. I didn't want to make a pig of myself.

I went on like that for about eight months. Binge on steak, purge on salad. Binge on ribs, purge on Styrofoam peanuts. And it worked. I wasn't feeling that good, but I sure was looking good.

Then the holidays came. I don't know who started this evil tradition, but for some reason everybody decides that Christmas is the time to send sweets. I'd come to work every day, and there would be another plate of cookies, another box of caramel popcorn, another cherry pie. They should have just made it easy and sent me a bag of sugar and a bucket of lard, let me suck it up with a straw.

Those Christmas sweets, they broke me. They absolutely

broke me. Jennifer would walk by and see me eating a piece of pie and she'd say, "That's all right, Rodney, but just one. You're on a diet."

I'd say, "This is three."

"You ate three pieces of pie?"

"No. I ate three whole pies."

"Well, shit, Rodney."

"I wish I could, Jennifer. I wish I could."

CHUCK E. CHEESE

areful now, because I'm about to lay a really heavy cliché on you. The most important thing in life is . . . titties.

All right, you caught me. It's not titties. It's family.

I know because I spent two years in Hollywood with a fake family. I had the blond wife, the best friend, a couple of boys. And I hated it.

I did a spread for *In Touch* magazine. They came out and took a picture of my house in Los Angeles: "This is how he lives!" But it wasn't my house. It was just the house I rented and filled with rented furniture.

They wanted to take a picture of me wrapping Christmas presents, but I didn't have any Christmas presents. So they went out and bought me some. "Stand there. Hold a Christmas cookie. Act like you're enjoying the Christmas coffee." It was a fantasy life. *Look at him. He's wrapping his presents and eating his cookie and drinking his coffee, just like you. He's Rodney "Perry Como" Carrington!*

My family is my life. The greatest moment of my life

wasn't getting a television show; it was marrying the woman I got pregnant when I was twenty-three, even though I'd only known her six weeks. I was homeless, I was broke, and I was very, very focused on my career. I was willing to do whatever it took to make it in comedy—drive thousands of miles, sleep in my truck, live for years and years without a penny to my name. You can't really do that with a wife and kids.

But I didn't have a father growing up, and I couldn't imagine a woman raising my children without me around. So I married that woman. We had more kids. And I found out that the career I always wanted wasn't nearly as important as the kids.

Not that it's easy to be a parent. It's hard. Every damn day. I've got a twenty-foot drop-off in my backyard that goes down to a creek, so I hung a board from a thirty-foot rope so we could swing right out over that creek. Daddy got on to try it first, and my god, it was exciting. Then I looked down and realized it was fifty feet to the ground. Suddenly, it was terrifying. That's what parenting is like.

I got back on solid ground and said, "Don't swing on that swing. It's scary as hell. You could be killed. Daddy's going to get a saw right now and cut down the rope. Then I'm going to cut the whole limb off that tree just for good measure."

I look out the window twenty minutes later, and my kids are out there swinging on that rope swing. Scared the hell out of me. Scared the hell out of them, too.

That was a year ago. Look out in my backyard right now, and what do you think you'll see? You got it. That rope swing is still hanging from that tree branch.

I love those boys. They're fun. But that doesn't mean I don't want to kill them. You can't take three kids to the Dairy Queen without something going haywire, much less give them boxing gloves for Christmas. Which I did. Big mistake.

Christmas morning. Wrapping paper everywhere. My wife's

on the couch with the video camera. My dog Poopie's over by the fire. The Christmas tree is up, Christmas music is playing—"Silver bells, silver bells"—it's real nice fighting music, so I get the boys all decked out in their new boxing gear. I put on my boxing gloves, get down on my knees, and says, "Merry Christmas, boys. Everybody gets to fight Daddy."

George gets up first. He's seven. Tiny. He starts hitting me and I'm laughing and giggling. "You really working Daddy over, big boy. That's good punching."

Next comes Sam. He's ten. He starts really hitting me. Now everybody else is laughing, but I'm really trying to block those punches because he's swinging hard.

Then comes Zach. He's twelve. I'm still down on my knees, so he's a foot taller than me. I'm laughing, swaying back and forth, "All right, Zach, here we . . ."

Bam. He hit me right in the nose. Hard. The next thing I know I'm up off my knees and I've pushed poor Zach across the room. "You don't hit Daddy like that. That hurt. Am I bleeding, honey? I'm bleeding. I know it. I think he broke my nose. What the hell is wrong with you? It's Christmas!"

I was crying. Zach was crying. The dog was barking. My wife stopped filming and took all the stuff away from us. It ruined Christmas. Just ruined it.

Two weeks later, to make up for the boxing, I voluntarily, without being begged, took my kids to Chuck E. Cheese on a Saturday night. If you are considering kids, go spend a Saturday night at Chuck E. Cheese You will leave there and buy a dog instead, I guarantee it.

For those of you without kids, Chuck E. Cheese is a pizza-serving hell house full of video games, ball pits, climbing tubes, and a robot band featuring a mouse, a gorilla, and I think a vampire but I'm not sure. There are kids everywhere, screaming, and at least three of them throw up every hour from the

overstimulation. And the worst thing is, Chuck E. Cheese lim-
its you to two beers. That's enough to get you edgy, but not
enough to dull the pain.

Of course, the real reason I agreed to go is because of the
skee-ball. I love that game, and I'm damn good at it. Got my
own set of balls. Got some special shoes, too. I'm even in a
league on Tuesdays. It's kind of like bowling for idiots.

Last time I was in Chuck E. Cheese, I played skee-ball for
seven straight hours, won every game. I got 10,418 tickets
and took them up to the front desk to score me some loot. I
whipped out that big roll and said, "Give me that plastic pocket
comb, a troll pencil, and a spider ring. How much I got left?"

"Thirteen tickets."

"Thirteen tickets!" I looked around. Some other dad was up
on stage, fistfighting that gorilla. He finally went completely
nuts and ripped the gorilla's head off. He just couldn't take it
anymore. That's what Chuck E. will do to you if you haven't
been keeping up with your conditioning.

But I was a pro. I called my son over and said, "George,
Daddy won these thirteen tickets playing skee-ball. Now I'm
giving them to you and you can get anything you want with
them."

He ate three of those tickets before I'd even stopped talking. But I loved him for it. I really did. When you love your
kids, you love them even when they do something stupid. I was
sitting in the living room watching television one day, and my
middle son, Sam, who was about two at the time, came walking in and pooped on the carpet like a horse. I'm serious. Two
brown circles fell out of his butt. He looked at me as if to say,
"Yeah, so what? What are you going to do about it?" and just
kept walking.

I wrote that incident into my comedy. In the act, I whip him
with a newspaper and rub his nose in it. But that's not what

really happened. What really happened is that I just sat there. I couldn't believe it. My first thought was . . . *That's nasty. Where's my wife? She needs to clean that up.*

But then I thought about that look he gave me, kind of cocky, kind of cool, kind of annoying as hell. I thought, *My god, that boy is just like me.*

DOWN WITH THE CLOWN

One of the most important things you can do as a parent is joke with your kids. They're so honest and sincere, it's almost like shooting fish in a barrel, which I tried once; it's not as easy as it sounds.

I take great pleasure, as a father, in embarrassing my kids. One of my favorite places to embarrass them is at a restaurant. The waitress will come up and I'll say, "Hi. I'll have the mountain oyster sandwich with relish, a side of fries, and my son thinks you're pretty."

"Dad, no I don't!"

"You don't think she's pretty?"

"No!"

"Son, that is rude. Tell the waitress you're sorry."

It's even better when they try to do it back to me. They'll say, "I'll have the chicken fingers and a chocolate milk and, um . . . my dad likes you."

"Yes, I do. You're doing an excellent job."

"No, Dad. You want to marry her."

"I'm sorry, ma'am. I do like you, but I'm already taken. But my son is available. Did you know he doesn't even have a girlfriend?"

"Dad!!!!"

I leave an extra-big tip, then take the kids to the batting cage. They're all huddled down by the plate, batting helmets too big for their little heads, bats almost too heavy to swing. I turn the machine up to 90 mph, which is the highest speed.

"All right, kids. Step back a little and get a good look at what this is going to be like."

The ball goes by them so fast it hits the back fence before they even have a chance to turn their heads. My oldest, Zach, who is twelve, says, "No, Dad, it's too fast. It's too fast, Dad."

"No, no, it's fine. You can hit that."

"No, Dad, it's too fast. It's way too fast."

This works because from the ages of nine to twelve your kids think you are a complete idiot. They act like they are the smartest beings on the planet, and you just arrived from Pluto yesterday. But they're still innocent little kids, so they never realize you're just fooling with them.

So I work that angle. My oldest boys are at the age where they've got their own slang at school, so I play along. I'll see them all hanging out, watching television, and I'll come in and say, "Hey, boys, you down with the clown?"

"Dad, what are you talking about?"

"You know, are you down with the clown?"

"What is that? What are you saying?"

"I'm hip. I'm saying my stuff. I'm doing my thing."

"Dad, that's nothing."

"All right, well, if you guys aren't down with the clown, I guess . . ."

"Dad, you're not even saying anything."

"Maybe you just think that because you don't know. You're not with it."

"No, Dad, that's stupid."

"Well, you down with the clown, Zach?"

"No!"

"You down with the clown, Sam?"

"No!"

"George, are you down?"

George is seven, so he still wants to be on Dad's team. "Yeah, Dad, I'm down with the clown. Can we get some ice cream?"

Enjoy those moments of innocence while you can, people, because it don't last long. Right now, I'm way ahead of my kids. I'm thinking circles around them. But when they turn thirteen, they're going to be a whole lot smarter than I am.

THE END OF THE SIX-PACK

Let's see: whiskey, Wal-Mart, Disney World . . . I've led a pretty full life. I certainly can't complain. Sure, I've been complaining throughout the book, but I really shouldn't complain, because I've gotten everything I've ever wanted out of life except a movie deal, a chicken corndog, and a stint in Folsom Prison so I can be like Johnny Cash. But I'm in my thirties, I travel regularly to Reno, there's still time.

Yep, I've led a good life, and my wife, Terri, has been through it all with me. She's been there with me for every scary moment and every big event. She's like a rock. In my shoe. That I can't get rid of.

She's the person who always reminds me, "To hell with them if they can't take a joke." Terri was with me the first time I did *The View.* Me and Barbara Walters and all those women. I was scared to death. Terri said to me, "Rodney, you belong here. Don't worry about it. You're going to be fine. You don't need to be nervous. I'm not nervous."

A producer walked up and said, "Ma'am, we'd like to put a microphone on you in case we want to ask you a question."

Terri looked at me and said, "I think I just shit myself." And she had. I smelled it. She was that scared.

It's hard to believe, but we've been married thirteen happy years. Seven for her, five for me, and one year neither one of us cared for.

It's hard to make a marriage work. Especially these days. There are too many temptations. Three billion women on the planet, six billion boobs. That ain't even fair.

Adam and Eve had it easy. One man, one woman, one set of boobs, one rule: Don't eat the apple. Hell, even I could have handled that.

God says, "Don't eat the apple, Rodney."

"Fine. Anything else?"

"Yeah. Don't put your wiener in her butt."

"What if I put the apple in there?"

"Long as you don't eat it."

But seriously, I thank God for Terri every morning of my life. It usually happens when I get out of the shower and look in the mirror. That's when I am reminded once again that I used to have a six-pack, now I've got a keg. I'm fat. I can't even hug myself all the way around. I can't even see my dick unless I bend over and meet it halfway.

Of course, fat and ugly can't stop me. I look around, close the door: helicopter, helicopter, helicopter.

Baby Back

Darling, when we met you were a pretty thing,
but your body started changing when I gave you that
   ring.
You're supersizing, no exercising, good-bye working out.
A double meat with cheese, another helping please,
baby that's what you're all about.

I picked you up in my pickup truck
But you had to ride in the back.
I stopped off at the sonic burger
And you ate everything in my sack.
Darling, please, won't you please think of me.
I'd love to have my baby back, my baby back, my baby
   back.

Six months have passed and you've gained fifty pounds
And I confess, you've got a real big rack.
But the bad part is, when I give you a hug,
You got two more on your back.
You're supersizing, no exercising, good-bye working out.
A double meat with cheese, another helping please,
Baby that's what you're all about.

I played football with the boys last night
And you were all-time quarterback,
But none of us could tackle you,
'Cause you're built like a lumberjack.
Darling, please, won't you please think of me.
I'd love to have my baby back, my baby back,
Put down the ribs, and baby come back to me.
Baby won't you come on back.

SQUIRRRRREL

What happens after thirteen years of marriage? I'll tell you. Complacency sets in. Fun leaves, the children start growing up, you settle into a family routine. The sex gets less and less and shorter and shorter and somehow you don't miss it. You look up one day and you're eating a double meat cheeseburger and a large fries with a doughnut on the side. And that's when you realize you just don't give a shit anymore.

If you are planning to fall back in love with your wife, take a look at yourself in the mirror. Naked. You don't stand a chance anymore. Especially with her.

And it's the best feeling in the world. It's freedom. Freedom from all the worry and the exercising and the caring about how you look. I think God invented heart attacks just to keep married men from completely letting themselves go. If it wasn't for the fear of a heart attack, we'd all be five-hundred-pound tubs of lard, sitting around all week with a bag of pork rinds and a case of beer, watching reruns of *Fish*.

Of course, it goes the other way, too. In the last few years, my wife's boobs have gotten longer. They used to be like soldiers at attention; now they're always looking down, unless they're lying down, and then one boob's looking off to one side, the other one's looking off to the other. I've got to grab them, look them in the nipple, and say, "Look at me when I'm looking at you."

Of course, my wife has an excuse. She's given birth to three boys. Going through that birthing process will make anybody sag. But does she really have to fart around me all the time?

She never used to do that. The first ten years we were married, I thought my wife was the perfect woman. She doesn't stink, she doesn't make noise, she doesn't even have any asshole, it just doesn't exist. Now she's a farm animal. She gets up in the morning and sounds like Tarzan blowing into a conch shell. Dogs come running up to our window. The neighbors think we're keeping a zebra in the backyard.

Actually, it's not that bad. My wife is a very clean, modest, and private person. She hates to smell bad, which she doesn't, by the way, and she hates to poot. Her twin, on the other hand, will burp and fart in front of anybody as loud as she can. She really is a farm animal. My wife is just the opposite.

Which is why it was so funny when her ass said "Squirrrrrel."

We were driving back from a restaurant called the Bistro in Tulsa, Oklahoma. I looked over at my wife. She seemed to be concentrating really hard, but I didn't pay much attention until something slipped out.

Terri didn't even look at me. She just reached over and turned on the radio like nothing had happened.

Smooth operator. Smooooth oper-a-tor.

But I'm her husband, by god, I'm not letting her off that easy. I called her on it. I said, "Excuse me, Terri, but did your butt just say 'squirrel'?"

She started laughing real hard. In fact, she started laughing so hard she farted again. The kids were in the back seat yelling, "Make her stop, Daddy, it stinks back here."

"Damn it, sons, I can't help it if she's a farm animal. The three of you contributed to that shit. And you ruined her boobs, too."

We stopped off at a convenience store just to air out the car. She came out with a gallon of milk and when she reached for the door handle I decided to play a little trick on her. I pulled forward a foot.

She laughed and said, "Stop it."

The kids are saying, "Do it again, Daddy. Do it again."

So I did it again. Terri wasn't as amused this time. She said, "You better stop that, Rodney, right this minute."

Uh-oh, it's on. She ran eight miles home, always just a foot away from finally grabbing hold of that door handle. After four miles, I rolled down the window and started taunting her. "How's it feel to get some exercise, honey? Break wind all you want out there, but don't be farting in my truck."

Dear penis,
I don't think I like you anymore
You used to watch me shave,
Now all you do is stare at the floor,
Oh, dear penis, I don't like you anymore.

It used to be you and me,
A paper towel and a dirty magazine,
That's all we needed to get by.
Now it seems things have changed,
I think you're the one to blame,
Dear penis, I don't like you anymore.

Now he sings . . .

Dear Rodney,
I don't think I like you anymore,
Cuz when you get to drinking,
You put me places I've never been before,
Dear Rodney, I don't like you anymore.

Why can't we just get a grip
On our man to hand relationship?
Come to terms with truly how we feel.
If we'd put our hands together,
We'd just stay home forever,
Dear penis, I think I like you after all.

Oh, and Rodney, while you're shaving,
Shave my balls.

THE LETTER

Ibelieve in a little mystery in a marriage. Not if someone spends three hundred dollars on a purse, that shouldn't be a mystery, but five hundred on a fishing pole, nobody needs to know about that now, right?

Mystery is important, but after years of marriage the mystery is gone. I know everything there is to know about my wife. I've seen everything she's got to show me. I don't even try to sneak up and look at her when she's in the shower anymore. Seeing a naked woman, even a gorgeous naked woman like my wife, is just not what it used to be.

Maybe that's what the song "Letter to My Penis" is all about. "Letter to My Penis" started out as just a funny idea. One day, I started thinking about peckers, and I realized that if there is one part of your body that knows something that nobody—none of your friends, not your wife—that absolutely nobody else knows, it's your penis. If he could talk, you would probably be in trouble. Let's be honest, if your penis could talk you would probably be in jail.

"Letter to My Penis" is about having a falling out with your best friend. It is about finding out your best buddy has betrayed you, and now you've got to sort this whole mess out. I was in my twenties when I wrote that song, so I figured the betrayal would be your penis blabbing some horrible secret to your girlfriend's vagina.

Now I realize that isn't the betrayal at all. The betrayal is that your relationship with your penis changes. You don't need him as much. You don't hang out like you used to. And he's jealous. He can't believe you can be happy without him. You used to get together every day to let off steam, now he's only there to run the water. And it hurts. It hurts him a lot.

But in the end, you and your penis come to an understanding. You're getting your excitement elsewhere (*Barney Miller* reruns on TBS), but you still love him. You still need him. Maybe only once a month, but it's still important. I still love you, penis. Come on now, you're my best friend. Give me a hug. Let's shake on it. And I tell you what, while I'm thinking about it, I'm going to shave your balls.

I'm a simple man. I drive real slow. I don't understand why people put spinning hubcaps on their wheels and purple lights under their cars. I think most teenagers are up to no good. At the end of the day, I like to sit on the porch with my wife and watch the sun go down. I'll reach over and grab her hand. She'll smile at me. My penis will start to get a little excited, he'll start thinking he's coming off the sideline, he's finally going to see some action . . .

And then the kids will come running out. George has a gummi worm jammed all the way up his nose. Sam bet him he couldn't get the whole thing up there but somehow he did it, and now it's time to be Mom and Dad again.

I get asked a lot, "Is your wife really like that? Is she really that cool?" Well, she let me write this book about her without once complaining *and* she still sleeps in the same bed with me. You make up your own mind.

SKIING IS FUN?

I thought after marriage, children, and Los Angeles, I had it all figured out. Then I went and did the dumbest thing I've ever done in my life: I took my family on a skiing vacation.

First, you have to buy $3,500 worth of ski clothes. A thin little T-shirt costs you $175 because it's made from Martian moonrocks that protect you from the cold and the wet. Honey, could you please explain to me again why I am going on vacation to a place that is cold and wet?

The first day at the ski resort is all about learning. I hate learning. When I'm on vacation, I don't want anything that is a mental or physical challenge. And it's not like I'm learning anything important. Eight hours, and all you learn to do is put on your boots and walk up a hill sideways. I couldn't sleep all night, I was so worried about getting up the next day and taking that test. If I was going to torture myself, I might as well have done something useful, like go to Mexico and take a Spanish class.

After two humiliating days, you're finally ready for the

slopes—and it is the biggest pain in the ass yet. You got to get your skis, you got to get your boots, you got to get your boots on, you got to get your skis on, you fall down, you fight the crowds, you wait an hour for the ski lift.

And the skiing is the worst part. The kids had no fear, of course, but the whole way down the slope all I thought about was the possibility of death. You hit one bump funny, you're off in the trees. If it can happen to Sonny Bono, why can't it happen to me? Sure, I'm going five miles an hour on the bunny slope, but that just means everyone in the lodge is going to see my hideous death and dismemberment. We were supposed to stay a week, but after two days I packed up the family and left.

We'll never go skiing again. I guarantee that. We're not ski people; we're beach people. We don't want something we have to learn; we want something we're already good at, like lying in an innertube, on the water, in the sun, drinking. The most thinking I want to do on vacation is wondering whether I should order a piña colada or a strawberry margarita from the swim-up bar.

Sure, I could die on a beach vacation, but what are the odds? The water is only three feet deep, and there are no sharks in the shallow end of the pool. The worst fate that could realistically befall me is sunburn or alcohol poisoning. And at least with those two I'll have fun getting there.

THE DOCTOR

I read the obituaries. I didn't want to admit it, but my friend Mark Gross called me on it enough times that I finally had to acknowledge it was true.

I'll sit down at the kitchen table with my coffee and my morning wood and start reading: Edward Koblinski, 87. Okay. Frank Villaponchorello, 92. Fine. Gertrude Stein, 73. Roger Barnstormer . . . 38!!! That's when I'll get mad.

> Roger Barnstormer, 38. Member of Calvary Baptist Church. Played the flute. Loved skydiving, chainsaw juggling, eating mushrooms he found in the woods, swimming with sharks, and solo treks across the North Pole. Died of . . . butthole cancer!

Oh, hell no, not butthole cancer. Anyone can get butthole cancer. That could have been me!

You've got to understand, I've never seen anything that I've done in my life as the end. I've never said, "Well, that's it. I've made it. I'm here. I can quit now." I can't imagine that happening because there are always bigger and better things ahead. That's the great wonderful weirdness of life.

But death's not like that. Death is the end. So I worry about dying. I'm a hypochondriac. If I stub my toe, I've got cancer, that's how serious it is. I bought a medical dictionary. Read the whole book cover to cover, found out I've got stuff I didn't even know existed. I've got rickets. And scurvy. What the hell is that?

This hypochondriac thing started about a year ago when I got a pain in my side. I told my wife, "It's not a tummyache. It's not gas. It's over here. It's cancer."

My wife just kept reading *Cosmopolitan* magazine, so I went to a medical professional. When that didn't work, I went to a doctor. The doctor told me to bring in a stool sample, but I'm an overachiever so I shit in a shoebox and handed it to him. He said, "Good god, I only needed a sample."

I said, "Get what you need and make a figurine off the rest. I ain't playing, doctor. I'm a desperate man. You're lucky I didn't put three of them on a stringer. You should have seen the one that got away. It broke the net. Now tell me about this pain in my side."

He said, "That's where your liver is."

Oh, God, not the liver. My liver and I don't have a good relationship. I've been having all the fun, and he's been stuck on cleanup duty for the last twenty years. If there's one organ that would want to take revenge on me, it's my liver.

The doctor poked me three times in the side, looked at my tongue, fondled my dick for some reason, and said, "It's nothing."

"You sure it's not cancer?"

"No."

"Shit. Don't tell me that."

"Don't worry, Rodney. We'll do an ultrasound."

"Ultrasound! I'm not pregnant. I must have cancer."

I looked up, and he was already gone. I went to the receptionist, and she told me I'd have to wait a few days. I said, "I can't wait a couple days. I could be dead by then. This shit is growing at a rapid pace. I'm noticing things I never noticed before, like wind and flowers and trees. I'm talking to bugs. I'm a basket case!"

Five weeks later, there's a woman scanning me with a little camera on a string and I'm crying like a four-year-old who's just shit his pants on the playground. She says, "How long have you had this?"

"For the love of God, what do you see?"

"Nothing. Now let go of my titties."

She took me down to another room for a CAT scan. That's where they slide you through a tube, look at all your insides, but before they do they make you drink a barium milkshake, which, by the way, is delicious. Three thousand bucks apiece, though. I think I'll just take a Frostee from Wendy's. It'll give me a brain freeze, you can poke all you want, I won't be able to feel anything for at least twelve minutes.

I got out the other side of that machine and the woman said, "We've got to check your prostate."

"Fine. Flip me over and slide me back through. I got all day."

Oh, no. It ain't like that. Two hours later I'm in the office with Dr. Woo-Woo. He's a Chinese fellow, about three feet tall. Which is good, because you don't want some six-foot fellow sticking his finger up your butt.

"Come on in here, Rodney."

"I don't think so, big fella. You take that Super Bowl ring off, and maybe we'll talk about it."

Two hours later he's coaxed me down out of the tree and

I'm in his office with my pants down. He puts a hand on my back and says, "Bend over."

"Keep your voice down, doc. There are people out there. I don't want them to know what we're doing in here. I don't even know you. So, um, what's your name? You come here a lot? You got any whiskey? It's my first time."

At that point, you start to wonder if there is something fishy going on. You don't even know if this is a real medical procedure. You've just heard about it from your buddies, and suddenly you think they might be putting you on. I mean, this thing is taking forever. It's not a quick process. There's no soft music. No candlelight. It's just a guy putting on a glove that goes all the way up to his elbow.

"Damn, doc, you don't need all that, do you? Is there a horse coming in after me?"

Then he asks you the stupidest question you've ever heard in your life: "Are you ready?"

"Am I ready? Am I ready? I've been crying all day, you sonofabitch."

Let's forget about the medical reasons and knock it down to the facts. You're in a room with a strange man, your pants are down, and he's got a glove on. You take the same situation and put it in a hotel room, and it's wrong. Very, very wrong. I know, because that's where the follow-up exam took place.

I walked out into the lobby of that hotel and everybody looked at me like they'd been watching it on the closed-circuit television. When I found out they had, I about died. I couldn't even drive home. I sat in my truck in the parking lot, my underwear in my pocket, crying.

I'm going to die of that butthole cancer, I guarantee it, because I'm not going back.

JUST TOSS IT IN THE CHILI

This year, I'm going to take a little bit of advice from my grandfather and not worry so much. When you're ninety, nothing bothers you. You don't have that much time left anyway, why worry about the little stuff? And whatever it is, it's always little.

"What's that lump on your neck, Grandpa?"

"Just a little cancer." He'll reach up and clip it off with his pocketknife. Put it in his mouth and give it a suck. "Not bad. Tastes like chicken."

My grandma called me the other day. She said, "Rodney, it's your grandma."

I said, "No shit, why are you whispering?"

"Your grandpa's asleep. Last time I woke him up, he made me mow the back pasture."

God bless that man. I can't even get my wife to vacuum the kitchen floor.

Grandma said, "Me and your grandpa went out shopping for caskets and funeral arrangements. We wanted to save you the trouble." Which is nice, because I won't even go near a casket. I'm so scared of caskets, I'd probably just throw everything off the side of the highway and be done with it.

How do you try out a casket? Lie down in it, see if you like the view?

"Hell, Flo, there's a nail in this one poking me in the back. This is bullshit. I can't lie on this for the next thousand years."

"Quit bitching, Harold, it's going to be a whole lot worse where you're going, you might as well get used to it."

They go down the next aisle and Grandma climbs into a sleek gray number. "Honey, do I look fat in this one?"

Grandpa's the practical one. "Is it cheaper if you get it shorter? If it is, y'all can just chop my legs off."

Then they try to sell you a hole for $10,000. I got an uncle that will give you an acre for $375, you can throw your whole family in there. You might get a little cowshit on your grave, but by God, you'll be with the people you love.

But first there's the funeral. I hate funerals. There's usually a dead guy there, and it's real uncomfortable. When the casket is open it's even worse, because I always see them move.

"He looks natural, don't he?"

"That's because he's not dead, jackass. I just saw him scratch his balls."

Everybody wants to look good when they're dead. Like they're sleeping. When I die, I want to look dead. I want to suck everything out of life and drop dead looking like I left nothing behind. I want people to say, "Thank God he went when he did. He looked like shit." I want them to walk by the casket and start gagging.

I don't want to be buried. I want to be cremated, thrown in the chili at the wake. I want everybody to have one last taste of the Rodsickle. But before they cremate me, I want them to cut my pecker off and throw that into the chili pot at the end.

Six words you don't want to hear at the wake: "There's a dick in the chili."

"There's a nut in there, too. If there's one, there's probably two. I ain't eating that shit."

I'm going to hell for that. I know it. I'm so sure of it I told my wife not to bury me in a sweater. Just put me in some flip-flops and a thong. I want to be ready for the fire. I want people laughing when I get to hell. I'm going to show up with a nut hanging out. "What's going on, people? Where's the oven? I am ready to tan."

If I do somehow manage to get to heaven, I'll probably be bottom rung of the angels. They'll give me a little tiny set of wings. I'll be flying around in circles like a wounded duck for the rest of eternity.

But I could be wrong. Maybe God really is the Great Mystery. Maybe he will open that big gold door in the sky and say, "Rodney Carrington, you funny sonofabitch. Get in here. Grab a beer. We've been waiting for you."

A SONG FOR WORLD PEACE

It seems to me this whole world has gone crazy,
There's too much hate and killing going on,
But when I see the bare chest of a woman,
My worries and my problems are all gone.
No one thinks of fighting, when they see a topless girl,
And maybe if you'd show yours, too, then we can save the
  world.

So . . .
Show them to me
Show them to me
Unclasp that bra and let those puppies free.
They'd look a lot better without that sweater
Baby, I'm sure you'll agree,
If you've got two casabas
Show them to me.

I don't care if they don't match or one's bigger than
    another.
You can show me one, and I'll just imagine the other.
Even if you're really old, there's really nothing wrong,
Don't be sad, it's not too bad, they're just a little long.

Show them to me
Show them to me
Lift up your shirt and let the whole world see.
Just disrobe and show your globes and a happy man I'll be
If you've got dos cha-chas,
(Which is Spanish for two titties)
Show them to me.

Don't be ashamed, don't be afraid, this show will not be
    rated,
Even if you've had thirteen kids, and you think they look
    deflated,
There's no such thing as a bad breast, I believe this much
    is true
If you're a big fat man I'm a titty fan, and I'd love to see
    yours, too.

Show them to me.
Show them to me.
Come on baby and let us see
All the world will live in harmony.
If you love your country . . .
I said, if you love your country . . .
Show them to me.

THANK YOU, GOOD NIGHT

So there you have it, people. You've wasted a perfectly good month of your life reading this book. I hope you've liked my brand of humor, and I hope you've laughed, and I especially hope that you've read this whole book without learning anything at all.

If you've done those three things, then I'm a happy man. Because I'm just here to make you laugh. I'm not here to change your moral values or fix anything. The last thing I want to do is to preach.

There is no message. There is no agenda. Drink your beer, laugh, have a good time. Drive safely on the way home. If you're reading this book on the pot, please be careful when you stand up. I don't want you to get lightheaded and go Elvis on us. After all, I might write another book one day.

Until next time . . .